Dressing with *Dignity*

"Who shall find a valiant woman? Far and
from the uttermost coasts
is the price of her. . . . She hath made
for herself clothing of tapestry:
fine linen, and purple is her covering. . . .
Strength and beauty are her clothing, and
she shall laugh in the latter day. . . .
Favour is deceitful,
and beauty is vain: the woman
that feareth the Lord, she shall be praised."
—Proverbs 31:10, 22, 25, 30

Dressing
with
Dignity

Colleen Hammond

SECOND EDITION

*"The queen stood on thy right hand,
in gilded clothing; surrounded with
variety."*

—Psalm 44:10

TAN BOOKS AND PUBLISHERS, INC.
Rockford, Illinois 61105

First Edition published in 2004 by Valora Media, Valley View, Texas. Second Edition published in 2005 by TAN Books and Publishers, Inc.

ISBN 0-89555-800-9

Cover design by Ken Henderson.

Colleen Hammond may be contacted for speaking engagements at Valora Media, Inc., P.O. Box 468, Valley View, Texas 76272. Tel. 866-299-2955. Website: www.ValoraMedia.com or www.ColleenHammond.com

Printed and bound in the United States of America.

TAN BOOKS AND PUBLISHERS, INC.
P.O. Box 424
Rockford, Illinois 61105
2005

This book is lovingly dedicated to
And placed under the protection of
The Immaculate Heart of Mary,
Our Lady of Fatima.

O Mary, conceived without sin,
Pray for us who have recourse to thee.

Acknowledgments

W E'VE experienced tons of devilish little incidents working on this project and have kept holy water close at hand constantly to sprinkle everything, and St. Benedict medals attached to everything too! I could write another book on all the ways "the dark side" has attempted to thwart this book via computer breakdowns, illness, accidents, etc.

But this page is the scariest part of the entire project, because I know I'm going to leave someone out!

So, to all of you that I have talked to about this project, or cried on your shoulder; to those who have encouraged me, have prayed, have emailed or have spread the word . . . THANK YOU!

Special thanks go to:

Dr. Alice von Hildebrand; our conversations a few years ago are what inspired me to write this book. I guess I'm a bit slow picking up God's hints. Your support and encouragement have meant the world to me.

The priests and theologians who combed over the manuscript for theological errors and prayed for this project.

The experts on Freemasonry and the occult who helped me with research materials and editing.

Mary Frances Lester for her support, encouragement and tremendously gifted editing.

Thomas A. Nelson, my publisher, for believing in the importance of this project.

Barb Stirling, who by her close friendship—and especially by her example—gave me the courage to keep on going, even through the pain.

Mark Kwasny, for his prayers, moral support and insightful suggestions.

Ken Henderson, for his intriguing cover and layout work.

Lu Cortese at St. Joseph Radio for her belief in me and for scheduling an "unknown" like me on her radio program.

The man who called *St. Joseph Radio Presents* the day I was a guest on the show and told me that God wanted me to write this book. I wish I knew your name, but I pray for you daily.

My favorite Saint, Blessed Anna Maria Taigi, whose example and "presence" in our home has brought us true peace.

My four lovable children. Without their encouragement, hugs, kisses and especially their loving prayers, I never would have started this project—let alone completed it. I love you all profoundly!

But most importantly, I want to thank my unbelievably supportive and saintly husband Dennis, whose idea it was for me to start writing and doing speaking engagements again. You gave me guidance and encouragement, you rubbed my shoulders when I was sitting at the computer. You brought me something to eat and drink in the wee hours of the morning when I was working on this book. You patiently endured my mood swings and frustrations. You read through all my rough drafts and offered great suggestions and clarifications. You always had a smile for me when frustration and anxiety got me down, and . . . well, this book isn't big enough for me to say enough good things about you.

Dennis, I love you.

—Colleen Hammond

How This Book Got Started

MY JOURNEY to modest fashions has been a very, *very* long one. I fell away from the Catholic Faith in college, when I really needed it the most. To put myself through college, I was modeling and acting—not the most Christian of industries.

The plan was to go to medical school (my undergrad work was in chemistry and psychology), but because of my modeling and acting background, I ended up working in television. I got a job doing the weather on The Weather Channel, so my husband and I moved to Atlanta. My best friend at the time was the Promotional Director for MTV, which gives you an idea of where I was in my life.

My return to the Faith is a long and tragic story, but when I did return, you wouldn't have been able to tell I was Christian by how I was dressing. I guess I thought real beauty was about how much of my form and body was exposed.

I abandoned my skyrocketing career the moment our first child was born. Due to a few disastrous events in our life that followed shortly afterward (you can hear the details on my reversion* CD entitled *The Making*

---

* "Reversion" means the return to the Catholic Faith of a fallen-away Catholic, analogous to *conversion* in the case of a convert.

of a Beauty Queen), we found ourselves broke. And I mean *penniless!*

We had only one car, which my husband took to work, so I didn't leave the house much. As a stay-at-home mother of one child (and an infant at that!), I had a lot of spare time on my hands.

I walked to the library one day and fumbled across a marketing study that the advertising industry had done in the 1970's. They had used modern technology to track a man's eyes when he looked at a woman wearing pants. The results of the study so shocked, sickened and disgusted me that I haven't worn pants in public since. (You can read more about the study in Chapter Three.)

At the time, my closet was full of slacks, tops, sweat pants and T-shirts. I didn't own a dress. This was going to be a radical change for me! Because we didn't have a dime to spare, I sewed myself one dress (it was too short) that I wore in public—that means to Mass, shopping, or to the park.

I started to read more about modesty, but the only books I could find at the time were not Catholic.

Somewhere, I got the idea that dressing modestly somehow meant plain, dreary, potato-sack type clothing. An Amish woman had more panache than the styles I started to wear! My new clothing choices were quite a departure from the chic outfits I used to wear when I was modeling and working in television.

Our marriage at the time was going through some changes and challenges, so I started reading books on marriage. Again, the only books I could find were not Catholic. With no other option, I started researching Catholic Church documents, looking for references to marriage, especially about that whole "you-must-obey-your-husband" thing.

My first book manuscript, *Love, Honor . . . and Obey?* is about the Catholic Church's teaching on wives' being subject to their husbands. I think that the Catholic teachings on the subject are much more beautiful and empowering for women than any other view out there.

I traveled the country interviewing people, doing conferences, helping re-build marriages and, I hoped, reaching souls. So many years of research and study had gone into the manuscript, and I was anxious to get it finished, approved by theologians and into bookstores.

But in March of 2004, I was a guest on *St. Joseph Radio Presents*, a live call-in radio program from the Los Angeles area heard on WEWN. God spoke to me that day in a powerful way. Why should I be surprised? He usually has to whack me with a two-by-four to get me to grasp what He's trying to tell me. This situation was no different!

My topic for the show was communication between men and women, building marriages, and of course my upcoming book, *Love, Honor . . . and Obey?* But every single phone call for two solid hours was from parents asking how to get their daughters to dress in a modest and dignified manner.

I still wasn't hearing God's message.

The last caller said, "Although I'm interested in your topic, Colleen, what I really think God wants you to do right now is to write a book on modesty."

It hit me like a ton of bricks! Looking back over the previous year, I had been asked to do many mother-daughter fashion shows around the country. Was teaching girls how to dress in a modest and dignified manner and develop their femininity more important right now than *Love, Honor . . . and Obey?*

I went to a local chapel to pray. Lying there on the pew was the book *Forty Dreams of St. John Bosco*. I flipped it open and it fell to page 34. My eyes went directly to this passage: "Don't you know that, where purity is concerned, *non datur parvitas materiae*—'there is no matter that is not considered to be grave'?"

Grave? Would that mean *mortal?*

I flipped through the book some more, and every page I went to had a passage having to do with the importance of innocence and purity.

Suddenly, every piece of the puzzle fell into place in my mind. Every sin against purity is grave, and that even includes our *thoughts,* right? I also realized that the male half of the world is extremely stimulated by what they *see*—through no plan or fault of their own. Now, considering what I've seen women and girls wearing to the store or the beach these days (not to mention what some wear to Mass!), it was clear to me that the caller was right. What is needed *right now* is a book about how to dress in a dignified, modest manner.

I went home and started researching. I was surprised at the amounts of material that were available from the Church but that I had never heard about. I was also shocked! It was amazing to see the sudden and rapid decline in fashions over the past 100 years. But what is so beautiful is how Heaven and Holy Mother Church have tried to warn us and keep us safe. The Church's role in warning us about increasingly degrading fashions has—unfortunately for women—been one of the best-kept secrets of the century.

Even though there is extensive information and material to share with you, my goal has been to keep the book short, sweet and to the point. Personally, I don't have time to read as much as I would like to. I have a pile of marvelous-looking books stacked next to my bed, waiting for me to read them. I can only imagine that you are in the same situation.

I've tried not to draw conclusions from the material presented here, but sometimes it's been hard to resist!

When I first read the information that is now contained in this book, and then looked into my closet, I realized how attached I had become to my own clothing, styles and outfits. I'm still weeding things out! I also realized how counter-cultural this information was going to be for most of us and that it may be difficult for others to toss out their favorite outfits too. *I promise you that the information here will give you something to think about—and lots to pray about!*

My hope is that you will read it, pray about it, and do what you feel is the right thing for yourself and your family, based on the facts presented here. May our Blessed Mother guide you!

It is my prayer that, within these pages, you are able to find the information *you* need to help you in your desire to dress with modesty and dignity and to inspire your daughters and granddaughters, god-daughters, nieces and other relatives and friends to do the same.

∽ Contents ∼

Dressing
with
Dignity

"I will greatly rejoice in the Lord, and my soul
shall be joyful in my God: for he hath
clothed me with the garments of salvation:
and with the robe of justice he hath covered me,
as a bridegroom decked with a crown,
and as a bride adorned with her jewels."

—Isaias 61:10

CHAPTER ONE

Out of Eden

"And they were both naked; to wit, Adam and his wife: and were not ashamed." —*Genesis* 2:25

NAKED and not ashamed? That's pretty hard to imagine.

I'll never forget the first time I read that passage from the Bible. I was a young girl growing up in Michigan, and the thought of being even half-dressed in front of anyone horrified me. To this day, the thought of being caught wearing a bathing suit in front of people gives me the willies.

A recent survey commissioned by the British women's magazine *REAL* showed that only 3% of women in the United Kingdom were happy with their own bodies.

> Of 5,000 women questioned, 73% said they thought about their size or shape every day. And six out of 10 women said their body image made them feel depressed . . . 91% of women were unhappy with their hips and thighs, 77% with their waist and 78% said they had cellulite.[1]

We women are pretty conscious of how we look, and I think it's safe to say that nearly all women would be ashamed to be seen naked in public. This is not only because our figures may be imperfect, but also (and more importantly) because of that whole thing with the Serpent and the fruit in the Garden of Eden.

But why weren't Adam and Eve bothered by their nakedness before the Fall?

Before Original Sin, Adam and Eve looked at each other with simple, pure, innocent love and with holy respect. St. Thomas Aquinas says that our first parents were innocent and in a state of "original justice."

So, what does it mean that Adam and Eve "were innocent and in a state of original justice?" Were our first parents goofy simpletons walking around the Garden of Eden with wide-eyed foolishness?

No way!

My parish priest explained it to me this way: When Adam and Eve came from the hand of God, they were gifted with Sanctifying Grace, so their souls were beautiful and pleasing to God.

Our first parents possessed all the virtues,[2] the seven gifts of the Holy Spirit,[3] and the twelve fruits of the Holy Spirit.[4]

In addition, Adam and Eve were infused with natural and supernatural knowledge, which means they knew everything they needed to know about surviving on a daily basis, and knew what they needed to know about God.

Our First Parents were not tempted by internal urges, as we are. They were free from concupiscence—that irrational desire for things that our bodies tell us we *want* but that our common sense tells us we really don't *need* . . . like the whole box of chocolate-covered cashews I crave when I'm pregnant! Their bodies easily followed the decisions of their wills. They would never have said, "I couldn't help myself!"

They also wouldn't experience sickness or even death, because they were immortal in both soul and body.

In other words, Adam and Eve were in the state of grace (no mortal sin on their souls), were loaded with virtue and with a degree of intelligence that would have put Einstein to shame, had great knowledge, weren't tempted by the promptings of the flesh (con-cupiscence), and they would never get sick or have to die. It must have been nice!

Life in the Garden of Eden before Original Sin was grand. It was . . . *Paradise*! Adam and Eve experienced no fear, no sadness, no regret, no mood swings, no dis-couragement, no temptation from within themselves.

Actually, St. Augustine said that Adam and Eve avoided sin "without a struggle."[5] Imagine avoiding sin without a struggle! Wouldn't that be fabulous?

Which brings us to the other wonderful quality they possessed: reverence.

Reverence is respect, admiration, awe, veneration and amazement. It means showing honor, respect, con-sideration and appreciation for God Himself, for God's creation and for each other.

Reverence includes also the idea of a "holy fear"—a fear of not pleasing God. A fear of not *being* pleasing to God. Scripture says, "The fear of the Lord is the beginning of wisdom." (*Psalms* 110:10). Those who are reverent also know when to express their feelings, when to hold them back, and aren't carried away by them.

Sadly, our society has lost the concepts of reverence and respect. Let me give you some examples.

Some people have absolutely no sense of reverence for the Blessed Sacrament. After Mass, there are folks who chat or even shout across the pews in church to their buddies, seemingly oblivious of Our Lord's being present in the Tabernacle. They are also insensitive to those people who are kneeling and praying their thanksgivings after Mass. A number of people don't genuflect when passing in front of the Tabernacle, and some children aren't even sure why we genuflect in the first place!

What about our loss of respect and reverence for each other?

Whatever happened to simple manners and common

courtesy? To the Ancient Greeks, good manners and high morals were the same thing. Whereas we today may consider an unmannerly person simply "rude," the Ancient Greeks would have considered an impolite person *immoral* and *filled with vice*. They understood that a person's inner character is revealed by how he or she behaves.

It's rare these days to see men holding doors open for women, or to hear "please" and "thank you." Our family now lives in the South, where it's still common to hear "Sir" and "Ma'am," where men still hold doors open for ladies and try not to use coarse language when a lady is present. It's refreshing. But overall, chivalry in our society has certainly taken a beating.

For example, many men I know have met with hostility when holding a door open for a lady. My girlfriend's son says that when women give him a hard time for holding the door open for them, and they sneer, "Don't you think I can handle it? Are you only holding the door open for me because I'm a *woman*?" he'll politely answer, "No, I'm holding the door open for you because *I'm a gentleman*." (Good answer, eh?)

These days, it is difficult to be chivalrous—but not impossible!

Brad Miner wrote in *The Compleat Gentleman* that a chivalrous man has

> . . . an attitude, an interior commitment . . . to a way of life that values the martial skills used to defend the true and the beautiful, the passionate respect for true and beautiful women, the erudition necessary to comprehend true and beautiful ideas, and withal the serenity necessary, no matter what, to remain composed.[6]

A chivalrous man is valiant, honorable, generous, courteous, and gallant. And *Merriam-Webster* says he is "marked by gracious courtesy and high-minded consideration, especially to women."[7]

Teaching our young men to be chivalrous gentlemen will help rebuild respect for life and for others—which brings me to my next point.

What about how our elders are treated? There was a time when the older generation was treated with respect. Youth would approach their elders for advice, realizing that Grandma and Grandpa's decades of life experience had given them wisdom.

Instead, our culture treats seniors as people who are past their prime, as if they had an expiration date. Sometimes they are needlessly put into retirement or nursing homes, and sometimes family members consider euthanizing them. This lack of respect—irreverence, if you will—for our elders waltzed blatantly through my life a few months ago.

I was coming home from the grocery store with my four children. As I drove past the entrance to the store on my way out of the parking lot, I saw a frail, elderly woman leaning on the trunk of a car in the handicapped parking spot. Another woman, whom I later found out was the frail woman's older sister, was struggling to get a wheelchair out of the trunk of their car.

I was about to get out of my car and help them, when I saw a middle-aged man approaching the store from the parking lot. He was looking directly at the two elderly women and could easily see that the sister was still struggling to remove the bulky wheelchair from her trunk. The man continued to look at the elderly women as he strode past them and right into the grocery store.

I was dumbfounded!

At that moment, another man came out of the store. Surely he would help the two elderly women. Although he clearly saw the feeble woman struggling with the wheelchair, he too walked past!

That was it! I wasn't going to wait any longer.

With tears in my eyes, I climbed out of the car and helped the women. I easily lifted the wheelchair out of the trunk, locked the wheels, helped the woman into the seat, then pushed her up the ramp into the store.

Have we really lost that much respect for our elders? Or is it because we women have too often in recent years brushed off men's offers to help with an "I am woman, hear me roar!" attitude? Have we conditioned chivalry out of our men? I think that's part of it. But that topic could fill another book by itself. Let's get back to reverence and respect.

How about the lack of reverence for human life? Slaughtering one's child has become a socially accepted "choice," instead of what it really is: murder.

Dr. Alice von Hildebrand in her book, *The Privilege of Being a Woman*, points out that the core of a woman's mystique is her ability to carry and give birth to a baby, which is the reason why females deserve such respect and reverence.[8] How beautiful!

To co-operate with God and our husbands to create another living human being with a soul that will live forever is an awe-inspiring privilege. Wouldn't you agree?

Gertrud von le Fort wrote in *The Eternal Woman* that "To be a mother means to turn especially to the helpless, to incline lovingly and helpfully to every small and weak thing upon the earth."[9]

Is this why women who have had an abortion take so long to recover? I'm not the only one that thinks so.

> The diabolical work that has taken place since the legalization of abortion is that it has destroyed, in those tragic women who have allowed their child to be murdered, their sense for the sacredness of maternity. Abortion not only murders the innocent; it spiritually murders women. . . . the wound created

in their souls is so deep that only God's grace can heal it. The very soul of the woman is meant to be maternal.[10]

A woman who has had an abortion may not realize right away how deeply she has injured her God-given feminine vocation and how it has harmed her spiritually. As Mother Teresa of Calcutta said, when a woman kills her own child, she is not learning to love, but is learning to kill to solve her problems.[11] Depression, feelings of guilt, grief, rage, emotional numbness, eating disorders, low self-esteem, substance abuse and anxiety are all symptoms of Post-Abortion Trauma. (Referring such women to Rachel's Vineyard,[12] an organization that counsels women who have had an abortion, can be a great way to help them.)

We've seen irreverence displayed for Our Lord in the Blessed Sacrament. Every day, we experience a lack of respect for each other by an absence of manners. Generally speaking, our elders are no longer respected. There is no universal regard for an innocent, unborn child. And what about the reverence and respect due to our own bodies, that are temples of the Holy Spirit if we are in the state of Sanctifying Grace—our bodies that are intertwined with our immortal souls, which are created in the image and likeness of God?

Turn on the television these days, and you see matters of human intimacy treated as sources of humor. We hear the marital embrace being bandied about as a normal topic of conversation. We see sacred moments rendered as jokes on the afternoon and late-night talk shows. And worst of all, Hollywood emphasizes the marital embrace in a crass manner in movies aimed at teenagers. My husband tells me that, in today's workplace, many people (men *and* women!) chat about the marital act in the same breath as the NFL, their job or their family vacation.

And I think it's pretty obvious that the women's fashions of today are often geared toward destroying a woman's sensitivity for her femininity.[13] When did femininity become such an undesirable characteristic?

Dr. Alice von Hildebrand says that when women no longer know how to blush, it is an indication that a society is on the verge of moral collapse.[14] If this is true, it sounds like we're in a lot of trouble!

Dr. von Hildebrand also says that we women carry a heavy share of the guilt for the loss of respect for purity in our society. I agree. And if we don't treat *ourselves* with respect by dressing modestly, how can we expect others to do so? By dressing immodestly, we betray our feminine mission and vocation as guardian of purity that is given to us by God Himself.[15]

The comment I often hear is that societal norms dictate fashion. So, the argument goes, if it's usual for women to go topless in the wilds of Africa, then topless is perfectly modest in those parts of Africa.[16] Using this same argument, some people would say that if low-cut skin-tight jeans are the usual attire for women and teenage girls in the Western World, then low-cut skin-tight jeans are perfectly modest in the Western World. Yipes!

Of course, this amounts to having *no* standards, wouldn't you agree? Simple reason dictates that there must be some sort of yardstick to gauge things by— an absolute norm. The line must be drawn somewhere. But where?

Pope Pius XII addressed a Congress of the "Latin Union of High Fashion" in 1957 and spoke to this very topic.

> Yet, no matter how broad and changeable the relative morals of styles may be, there is always an absolute norm to be kept after having heard the admonition of conscience warning against approach-

ing danger: Style must never be a proximate [near] occasion of sin. . . .

It is often said, almost with passive resignation, that fashions reflect the customs of a people. But it would be more exact and much more useful to say that they express the decision and moral direction that a nation intends to take: either to be shipwrecked in licentiousness, or maintain itself at the level to which it has been raised by religion and civilization.[17]

That makes sense, doesn't it? Fashions express the direction the society chooses to take—and I don't know about you, but I'm not going to take fashion advice from a morally corrupt culture!

The *absolute norm* that the Pope refers to is this: If a fashion is an inducement to sin for others, it is a sin for us to wear it.

The term *proximate occasion of sin*—more commonly called the *near occasion of sin*—is basic Catholic jargon that Catholics used to learn in catechism class. So here is a review! Any person, place or thing that presents an allurement to sin is a *near occasion of sin*. A person is obligated to avoid near occasions of sin. (One is not obligated to avoid *remote* occasions of sin, which could include just about everything on earth.)

To wear the kind of clothing that can arouse unchaste thoughts or desires in others is to present them with a near occasion of sin. To wear that kind of clothing, *knowing* it has this potential, is a sin (either a mortal sin or a venial sin, depending on the degree of the immodesty and the other circumstances).[18]

So, for example, do low-cut skin-tight jeans on women and teenage girls present an allurement to unchaste thoughts and desires for the average male? Maybe we need some male input on this.

Many men (young and old) have written to me to

say that the answer is *Yes!* Matter of fact, I spoke with an 82-year-old man in Michigan recently who told me that he found it especially difficult at Mass because of what many of the young ladies and their mothers in the pews in front of him were wearing—especially when the females were wearing pants. He stressed that a man's age is not an issue when it comes to this kind of temptation.

Pope Pius XII refers to Our Lord's strong words about how it is better to cut off your hand or to pluck out your eye than to go to Hell. (*Matt.* 5:28-29). Then he states: "We must never yield, even in thought, to sin, and we must energetically repel anything that could so much as slightly tarnish this very beautiful virtue [purity]. In this matter, no care, no severity, can be regarded as excessive."[19]

Wow! The Holy Father goes on to say that the classic method of combating temptations to impurity is *flight* rather than fight.[20] Plus, he says that this struggle involves *constant vigilance*: "This watchfulness, extending to every moment and circumstance of our lives, is indispensable to us."[21] (The third classic Catholic ingredient of the struggle for purity is *grace*, which we can receive through prayer, Confession, Communion and devotion to the Blessed Mother.)

So, ladies, does this mean that good Christian men should *flee* from us if we dress immodestly? Are our "brothers" involved in a *constant struggle* for purity? (Or at least, *should* they be?) How often do we dress with their souls in mind?

Maybe we should be giving this matter more thought. Maybe we should be giving this matter more action! (We'll get back to this later.)

In our decadent and corrupt society, we've lost the sense of what is decent and what is not. Some mothers are thrilled that their daughters are only dressing like the pop star Madonna, and not like Britney Spears!

Pope Pius XII was dealing with what he considered a serious threat to the delicate virtue of purity in 1957 when he said:

> An excess of immodesty in fashion involves, in practice, the cut of the garment. The garment must not be evaluated according to the estimation of a decadent or already corrupt society, but according to the aspirations of a society which prizes the dignity and seriousness of its public attire.[22]

Think about what the fashions were in 1957! Pope Pius XII also stresses the importance of the intent of the designer. Do designers seek to create unchaste ideas and sensations through their fashion designs? How about the persons wearing the garments: do they desire to "look sexy"?

I used to model, and at times I was asked to wear some pretty sleazy outfits. By the grace of God, I never actually wore anything that I can now look back upon and regret wearing. But supermodel Kim Alexis had a different experience.

I learned about Kim's book from my friend, J. T. Finn, who publishes *Love Matters*. With his permission, I'd like to share with you the following from his newspaper.

> In case you don't know who she is, Kim Alexis appeared on more than 500 magazine covers, including *Glamour, Vogue* and *Sports Illustrated*. She was the Fashion Editor of "Good Morning America" for three years, and hosted "Healthy Kids" and "Ticket to Adventure with Kim Alexis" on cable TV.
>
> In her 1998 book, *A Model for a better Future*, Kim shares that as a supermodel, she was constantly asked to compromise her moral standards. "There are pictures I look back on today and think, Oh, why did I let them talk me into that? I made some choices I'm not proud of."

Kim also says in her book that many women are playing with fire in the way they dress.

> Dressing like a floozy tells the world, "Look at me, want me, lust after me. I'm easy and you can have me." Displaying intimate parts of the body is a form of advertising for sex—so if you dress to attract sexual attention, you can hardly blame anyone else if that kind of attention comes your way. But dressing modestly tells the world, "I respect myself and I insist on being treated with respect." It's possible to be stylish and attractive without wearing something that is too short, low-cut, or see-through.[23]

That's a supermodel's experience. But in my life as a mother of four in North Texas, I have also observed that when women are dressed in a feminine, modest and dignified manner, men will treat them with respect and consideration.

Clothing sends a powerful message. As the saying goes, you get only one chance to make a first impression! Pope Pius XII mentions the beautiful significance of the white garments worn by a child on First Communion Day, or by a young woman on the day of her marriage. He asks: "Do these not symbolize the totally immaterial splendor of a soul which is offering the best of itself?"[24]

On the opposite end of the spectrum, we've lost a sense of decorum in public today. It's tempting to dash to the store in whatever we happen to be wearing at the moment, because "everyone else is doing it."

At the grocery store, I've seen women in slippers and a robe (they could have been sick), women with curlers in their hair (it could have been an emergency trip for hair spray), and young men and women with their underwear hanging out of their pants (sorry, I can't come up with a valid excuse for that one!).

Even lawmakers felt the need to take action on that

last-mentioned situation, with the Virginia House of Representatives voting 60-34 to impose a fine on persons whose undergarments were visible above their pants or skirt![25]

Recently, my husband was helping our sons cut swords out of a slab of red oak. They needed a new blade for the saw they were using and asked me to run to the hardware store. I thought, "Should I just run to the store in my work clothes? Or should I change my clothes and fix up a bit?"

My parents taught me that it is a sign of respect for other people always to look your best in public. We are representing and honoring our family name, and our actions speak louder than words.

In the past, I have found that when I am dressed in a neat, modest and feminine manner, men will hold doors for me, help me find things in the store and offer to carry the items to the car for me. However, if I run to the store dressed in my work clothes, I am treated as "just another one of the guys." No one holds the door for me. No one helps me find what I need. No one offers to carry my purchases to the car for me.

So, before going to get the saw blade, I put on a nicer dress, a quick touch-up of mascara, and I fixed my hair. Guess what? The guy at the hardware store helped me find the saw blade. Not that I was fishing for his help or was trying to manipulate him, but more that it feels good to be able to help bring out the best in someone else.

Isn't it nice to see men who still have a sense of chivalry and treat women with respect? And what's wrong with allowing a man to fulfill his God-given role as protector and provider? Don't you think it shows a lack of humility when someone refuses another's help?

Why do you think men treat women differently when they are dressed femininely?

I believe it is because, subconsciously, men can read

women's body language. If they see a woman who dresses with dignity and who carries herself with grace and femininity, they pick up on that. They take it as a sign to approach her with the respect, reverence and honor a woman ought to have.

My male friends tell me that it is also much more enjoyable to talk with a woman who is dressed tastefully because they're not distracted by her body. Men tell me it's a challenge to talk to an immodestly dressed woman because they don't want to ogle, and so they have to force themselves to focus intently on her face.

Yet when a woman dresses with dignity, men tell me that this appeals to their chivalrous nature. Her femininity helps them to elevate their thoughts (not to mention their eyes). It allows them to uphold a woman's honor, to respect truth and beauty, and to grow in their role as a "gallant knight."

On the other hand, if a woman is dressed in an unfeminine manner, men are more likely to treat her like "one of the guys." If she is dressed immodestly, then they may view her as a sexual object and may even treat her in a crass manner. They certainly won't treat her with respect, and they may even verbally harass her.

I would guess that most women would rather be treated with respect. Doesn't it make sense, then, to fix yourself up a bit before going out? And isn't it also better for men to see women dressed in a feminine manner, so that it brings out the best in them too?

Instruction about modesty begins right from birth. Plato wrote that one of the aims of education is to teach the child ". . . to hate what should be hated, and to love what should be loved."[26]

Let's start teaching our children to understand and love the God-given differences between males and females, and to respect them. But how?

Little girls (and boys!) should be trained from infancy

to be pure and to respect the sacredness of their bodies. The importance of wholesomeness, innocence and purity should be continually ingrained in them as they grow up, especially as we must constantly counter the ideas that are being spread in our culture!

Modesty is instinctive (have you ever tried to give a bath to a child that is approaching the age of reason?), and we should support that good instinct, especially as our culture tries to desensitize us. That way, when our youth encounter impurity, they will recognize it for what it is and flee from it.

As Dom Lorenzo Scupoli advises in his *Spiritual Combat*, a person should not stick around and try to *fight* temptations against purity. Instead, we should *flee* from them, otherwise they will often conquer us. Remember King David?

Pope Pius XII told Christian (Catholic) mothers that they must "preserve intact that natural instinct of modesty" that God has given to their sons and daughters as a protection against impurity. He said that mothers must help their children pass through adolescence "like those who pick their way among serpents," so that their children will make it through that period "without losing anything of the joy of innocence."[27]

That's a tall order—especially in this day of music videos, scandalous TV shows, lewd songs on the radio, and the like. But would we Catholic mothers really want anything less for our precious children? (Teenagers like this *do* exist. I've met them, and these honorable and virtuous individuals are our hope for the future!)

The Pope went on to warn mothers not to let their children lose their sense of modesty through "indecency in dress."[28] This implies that a child has an instinct for modesty as part of his basic human equipment— but that this instinct can be lost if violated enough.

As parents, we have a huge responsibility in this regard. Pope Pius XII warned:

> O Christian mothers, if you only knew what a future of worries and dangers, of ill subdued doubts, of hardly suppressed shame you lay up for your sons and your daughters by imprudently accustoming them to live barely attired, making them lose the natural sense of modesty, you yourselves would blush, and take fright at the shame you inflict upon yourselves, and the harm which you occasion to your children, entrusted to you by Heaven to be brought up in a Christian manner.[29]

Pretty strong words! But he makes an important point. We should make the extra effort to clothe our children in a modest manner, right from the beginning of their lives. Archbishop Meyer of Milwaukee stated:

> Boys and girls must be taught as tiny tots to love modesty and must be corrected for immodesty. Even though they are too young to sin, they can and ought to be impressed with the beauty of modesty. Training in modesty is pre-eminently the function of the home, to be begun from earliest childhood.[30]

This sounds like an entire program of action. We Catholic parents have our work cut out for us!

It's really not that hard to find nice, feminine and modest clothing for toddlers. It is only when they get into the "girl" sizes that clothing gets risqué. But it's worth the effort to look for modest and feminine clothing, even for *little* girls. It's important that our girls learn to respect and treat their bodies in a pure and refined manner, right from the start. In Appendix One, I've listed places you can find modest, stylish and feminine clothing for yourself and your daughters. I also keep an updated list on my website.[31]

St. Benedict talks about the effect that our body language has on our souls.[32] He found that when someone kneels, bows and sits up straight at prayer (sound like your mother?), his soul is being trained to be more reverent as well.

The same is true of learning to be feminine. The more we practice, the more it becomes ingrained in our nature. Virtue, after all, is basically nothing more than a "good habit." And habits are formed by repeatedly doing the same things.

We are all creatures of habit, and we have a choice. Are we going to develop good habits with regard to dressing ourselves and our daughters? Or are we going to develop negative habits? When it comes to virtue, it's got to be one or the other. The choice is ours.

Feminine body posture for women includes learning to dress, walk and sit in a feminine manner. We need to make sure we do not cross our legs in a way that may be undignified or offensive. But I'll go into that in more detail in Chapter Five.

For now, we must re-learn reverence and respect (and teach it to our children!), because reverence and respect have been pretty much eradicated from our current generation and from our society in general. But re-introducing them is really not as tough as you might think.

NOTES

1. "Few Women 'Happy with their Bodies,'" BBC News, Nov. 5, 2002. http://news.bbc.co.uk/1/hi/health/2402363.stm
2. Principally, faith, hope, charity, prudence, justice, temperance and fortitude.
3. Wisdom, understanding, counsel, fortitude, knowledge, piety and fear of the Lord.
4. Charity, joy, peace, patience, benignity, goodness, long-suffering, mildness, faith, modesty, continency and chastity.
5. *De Civitate Dei,* xiv, 10.
6. Brad Miner, *The Compleat Gentleman* (Dallas: Spence Publishing Company, 2004), pp. 184-185.

7. http://m-w.com/cgibin/dictionary?book=Dictionary&va=
   chivalrous
8. Alice von Hildebrand, *The Privilege of Being a Woman* (Ann
   Arbor: Sapientia Press of Ave Maria University, 2002), p. 87.
9. Gertrud von le Fort, *The Eternal Woman* (Milwaukee: Bruce
   Publishing Co., 1962), p. 78, cited in von Hildebrand, *op. cit.,*
   p. 96.
10. Alice von Hildebrand, *op. cit.,* p. 96.
11. "But I feel that the greatest destroyer of peace today is abor-
    tion, because it is a war against the child, a direct killing of
    the innocent child, murder by the mother herself. . . . By abor-
    tion, the mother does not learn to love, but kills even her own
    child to solve her problems. . . . And, by abortion, the father
    is told that he does not have to take any responsibility at all
    for the child he has brought into the world. That father is
    likely to put other women into the same trouble. So abortion
    just leads to more abortion. Any country that accepts abortion
    is not teaching its people to love, but to use any violence to
    get what they want. This is why the greatest destroyer of love
    and peace is abortion."
    http://www.priestsforlife.org/brochures/mtspeech.html
12. For more information, visit their website at
    http://www.RachelsVineyard.org.
13. Alice von Hildebrand, *op. cit.,* p. 90.
14. *Ibid.*
15. *Ibid*, pp. 84, 90.
16. See p. 125 below for St. Alphonsus Liguori's comments on this.
17. "Moral Problems in Fashion Design: An Address of Pope Pius
    XII to a Congress of the Latin Union of High Fashion," Nov. 8,
    1957. http://www.sspxasia.com/Documents/CatholicMorality/
    Fashions.html
18. Fr. Heribert Jone, O.F.M. Cap., J.C.D., *Moral Theology,* 1961;
    Rockford, IL: TAN, 1993), nos. 145, 153 (pp. 85, 90). See also
    Fr. Lovasik (ref. in this note) and p. 57 below.
       Note: To wear immodest clothing (or to do anything else) *with
    the intention* of arousing unchaste thoughts or desires in any-
    one is a mortal sin. Cf. Rev. Lawrence G. Lovasik, S.V.D., *Clean
    Love in Courtship,* TAN rpt. 1974, pp. 10, 12, 28, etc.
19. Pope Pius XII, Encyclical "*Sacra Virginitas,*" Mar. 25, 1954,
    par. 51, from *The Woman in the Modern World* (Series: *Papal
    Teachings*), Selected and Arranged by the Monks of Solesmes
    (Boston: Daughters of St. Paul, 1959), Appendix II, p. 29.
       This book is cited hereinafter as *WMW.*
20. *Ibid.,* pars. 52-53, pp. 29-30.
21. *Ibid.,* par. 50, p. 28.
22. "Moral Problems in Fashion Design," *op. cit.*
23. Quoted from *Love Matters* (Redondo Beach, CA, Vol. 8, 2004,
    p. 5), which is available at http://www.lovematters.com/, or by

calling 1-800-858-3040. (Note: This publication strives to promote chastity and prevent abortions through interviews on sexual topics with various celebrities. Though published by Catholics, it is intended for distribution on secular college campuses and does not always use traditional Catholic reserve when treating of sexual matters. —*Publisher,* 2005.)

24. Pope Pius XII, "Allocution to the International Congress of Master Tailors," Sept. 10, 1954, par. 450, in *WMW*, p. 232.
25. The vote took place on Feb. 8, 2005. "'Droopy drawers' bill seeks end to overexposure of underwear in public," *The Washington Times*, Feb. 14-20, 2005, p. 4.
26. Plato, *Laws II*, 653, cited in von Hildebrand, *op. cit.*, p. 69.
27. Pope Pius XII, Allocution to Mothers, Oct. 26, 1941, par. 97, in *WMW*, p. 76.
28. *Ibid.*, par. 98.
29. Pope Pius XII, Allocution to the girls of Catholic Action, May 22, 1941, par. 67, in *WMW*, p. 60.
30. Most Rev. Albert G. Meyer, S.T.D., S.S.L., Archbishop of Milwaukee, "Decency and Modesty" (Pastoral Letter), May 1, 1956, par. 24. (The Archbishop later became Cardinal Meyer of Chicago.)
31. www.ColleenHammond.com
32. Alice von Hildebrand, *op. cit.*, p. 90.

CHAPTER TWO

A Return to Reverence and Respect

C AN you think of a time when you have had a "reverent response" to God or to His creation? Sunsets are a beautiful example. Have you ever seen one that took your breath away? Or gazed out at the ocean and couldn't take your eyes off the tumbling waves? How about the glory and majesty of a mountain view?

Isn't it wonderful to admire something that deserves our admiration, awe and reverence?

In their innocence and state of original justice, Adam and Eve always responded with reverence to the greatness, beauty and dignity of being, whether it was to God, to God's creation, or to each other.

Adam and Eve regarded each other with a holy respect and took simple, pure and joyful pleasure in each other's company. At the same time, they did not experience sadness, fear or anger. A perfect situation, if you ask me!

But how different we are after Original Sin! We are now tempted by the things of the world. Women are often tempted by their emotions, but men are wired differently. Guys are greatly affected and tempted *by what they see!*

God told man to subdue the earth (*Genesis* 1:28), so men are usually too busy "sweating by their brow" (*Genesis* 3:19) to get involved emotionally with every woman they are attracted to. But their minds can quickly go from working to physical desires. Men constantly struggle with bodily temptations—something easily aroused by the women they see, if these men do not exercise what is called "custody of the eyes." As a woman, I don't understand this . . . but I have learned to *respect* it.

So what exactly is "custody of the eyes"? We women can't relate to it in the way that it applies to men (just as men can't relate to PMS). So let me give you some examples.

Have you ever thought about what causes your heart to beat? Why your mouth waters when someone talks about your favorite food? Why you shiver in the cold, blink your eyes when a foreign object comes near them— or even about what starts the birthing process? All of those involuntary activities are controlled by your "autonomic nervous system." They are going to happen whether we plan them, desire them, want them to, or even *don't* want them to!

When there is a "change in the environment"—a stimulus of some kind—your body automatically responds. If you accidentally touch a hot stove, your hand jerks back. If someone jumps at you out of a dark alley, your "fight or flight" reflex kicks in. The hormone adrenaline is automatically released, your heart races, muscles tense, and pupils dilate. Did you plan that hormonal reaction? No! It happened automatically.

These automatic reactions are not intellectual or "knowing powers," but instead simply "blind reactions to stimuli." These reactions are responses of our "sense appetites" ("sensitive appetites") or "passions," also known as the "emotions."[1] Our passions can take on a life of their own and "assume a dangerously independent role with respect to reason."[2] Basically, our emotions can get in the way of clear thinking.

> . . . not only does pleasure, if not properly con-
> trolled, operate irrationally, but it directly impedes
> the functioning of reason. More than simply dis-
> tracting us from the reasoning process, pleasure
> boldly intrudes upon that process and interrupts its
> proper workings. If pleasure becomes the dominant
> and ruling factor in our lives we simply cannot think
> straight. It is not that in such a circumstance there
> is a complete cessation of thought, but that the right
> roles of reason and passion are reversed. Reason
> becomes a sycophant to pleasure, and what think-
> ing is done is done mainly in the service of
> pleasure.[3]

So what should we look out for? St. Thomas Aquinas
has defined the eleven basic human emotions that will
automatically react to the changes in our environment.
They are love, hate, desire, aversion, pleasure, pain,
hope, despair, courage, fear and anger.[4]

Let's take fear, for example. "Fear cannot help but
respond worrisomely to what is perceived as fearful."[5]
I have an irrational fear of spiders. I know they are
tiny little things that are easily squashed with my
foot. So why does my heart race every time I see one?
I try to control my fear and smash the household
intruder.

So our goal in life is to make sure "our will is rul-
ing [our] passions"[6] so that our passions can be of good
service to us.

For us gals, our emotions are tough to control . . .
especially when we add in hormones!

For men, their hormones automatically react to
changes in their environment and can be tough for
them to control too! They see a female dressed in a
provocative manner and their autonomic nervous system kicks in. They're aroused. Not because they *want*
to be, but because their bodies automatically release
hormones that cause the arousal. God has given men

this reaction to help insure the survival of the human race, but they have to control it and use it for the purpose that God intended.

Men cannot control the fact that the arousal has happened, but they *do* have control over *how they will respond to it!* Will they turn their eyes away and fire a quick prayer to Heaven? Or will they succumb to lustful thoughts?

Can we just say, "It's his problem, not mine"? One woman addresses this question:

> Radical feminism insists that if a man has immoral thoughts because of the way a woman is dressed, it is *his* problem, not hers. Contrary to what these militants claim, males and females *are* different. Men are by nature more inclined to sensual reactions from visual stimuli, and women who dress in provocative ways bear some of the responsibility if their immodesty leads a member of the opposite sex to immoral thoughts.[7]

This author goes on to present a priest's explanation:

> Because traditional Catholic teaching on modesty in the area of sexuality requires the woman to keep more of her body concealed than it does for the man, some Catholics believe that it is unfair to the woman. While it is true that traditional Catholic teaching on modesty in the area of sexuality is more demanding of the woman, it is not unfair. Just as the woman is the weaker gender in the area of physical power, so the man is the weaker gender in the area of sexuality (in the sense that the male is more prone to immediate sexual arousal). And just as it is wrong for a man to use his physical strength to lord it over a woman, so it is wrong for a woman to use the feminine characteristics of her physical body to dominate a man.[8]

But that wasn't the way it was with Adam and Eve before Original Sin, according to St. Thomas Aquinas. Their love for each other didn't include lust.

Then that tricky old Serpent started talking with Eve . . . and she chatted back. What was she thinking?

The Serpent—the great liar—duped Eve, and she crumbled before the sin that comes before every fall: pride. First, she gave in to the devil in thought. *Then* she sinned by the action of eating the fruit. St. Augustine says that "the woman could not have believed the words of the serpent, had she not already acquiesced in the love of her own power, and in a presumption of self-conceit."[9]

Eve tempted Adam with the Forbidden Fruit, and Adam accepted it. The rest is history.

Because of Original Sin, Adam and Eve lost that grace which makes us holy and pleasing to God—Sanctifying Grace.[10] Their eyes were opened to the knowledge that they had brought upon themselves the dreadful evil of sin.

Their flesh didn't easily obey their will anymore. St. Augustine says that as soon as they disobeyed God's command and gave up Sanctifying Grace, "they were ashamed of their nakedness, for they felt the impulse of disobedience in the flesh, as though it were a punishment corresponding to their own disobedience."[11]

All of a sudden, Adam and Eve looked at themselves and exclaimed, "Whoa! We're naked!" And at the same time, they were ashamed.

Ashamed? Why? They hadn't been ashamed before.

It was because they realized that they were no longer pleasing to God. They were "stripped" of Original Justice. They were "naked" of Sanctifying Grace. They were now subjected to all the miseries and evils that you and I experience every day. And this was a shocking change for them.

Now they would suffer hunger, cold, sickness and death. They lost the supernatural virtues, the gifts of the Holy Spirit and the fruits of the Holy Spirit. Suddenly, it was hard to learn, and often even harder to remember!

They also lost their integrity. Unexpectedly, they were tempted by the world around them, tempted by the cravings of their bodies, tempted by the devil. Temptations now acted on the new weaknesses in their souls.

More powerful than an atomic bomb, Original Sin demolished the order of what was important and what was not. Power, success and accomplishments became overvalued.[12] That can be plainly seen in Ancient Greek literature, which glorifies "strength, accomplishment, courage and power." (Try Homer on for size!)[13]

We see the same mix-up in values in our current culture, too. Secular society glamorizes sports and idolizes professional athletes. "Power, riches, fame, success and dominance are idolized; humility, chastity, modesty, self-sacrifice and service are looked down upon as signs of weakness."[14] Talk about turning values topsy-turvy and bringing on anarchy!

Along with all this disorder, femininity and motherhood have been cheapened, and lust has entered the picture. Advertisers recognize this development, and they take advantage of it every day! Have you seen the seductive T.V. ads lately? And how about the sexuality blatantly shown in beer commercials? And all this from eating a piece of forbidden fruit!

To this day, using sexuality and seduction to attract and lure a man is a great temptation for certain types of women. Indeed, some gals are really good at it! They will use their feminine charms to trap a man and manipulate him, in order to get what they want from him. And it's usually money! "For the lips of a harlot are like a honeycomb dripping, and her throat is smoother than oil." (*Proverbs* 5:3).

Have you ever wondered why some women dress in a sexy and provocative manner? I think it's safe to say that they want to attract attention to themselves, and maybe they think they're being admired when they dress that way. But I've heard many men comment that if a woman is not for sale, then why is she advertising? Holy Scripture even says, "Behold a woman meeeth him in harlot's attire, prepared to deceive souls." (*Proverbs* 7:10).

Holy Scripture has an extreme example of women using their feminine charms to manipulate a man: Herodias and her daughter Salome. The mother schemed. The daughter danced. And together they tricked King Herod into giving them the head of St. John the Baptist on a platter. (*Matthew* 14:3-12; *Mark* 6:17-29).

How about David and Bathsheba? Granted, the Bible doesn't tell us that Bathsheba was *trying* to lure David. But he surrendered to her beauty and feminine appeal, and allowed his desire to have her as his wife outweigh his good sense and integrity. (*2 Kings* 11:1-27).

There are some positive examples in the Bible of a woman using her feminine charms for good, like Queen Esther and Judith. If you'd like a more modern example, think of Princess Diana in the early years of her marriage—how her grace and charm and impeccable feminine attire won her world-wide popularity, which she later used to focus world attention on hunger and other crying social issues.

Another great example of feminine charm was Mother Teresa of Calcutta. Remember her speech in Washington, D.C. on February 3, 1994? She charmed the world with her humility and straightforwardness. On that morning she said

> . . . And so it is very important for us to realize
> that love, to be true, has to hurt. I must be willing
> to give whatever it takes not to harm other people

and, in fact, to do good to them. This requires that
I be willing to give until it hurts. Otherwise, there
is no true love in me and I bring injustice, not peace,
to those around me.[15]

A woman who uses her feminine charms to get what
she wants from a man isn't showing any respect for
the personal human dignity of that man—or for her
own, either. She is acting sort of like a Black Widow
spider—which kills her mate after getting what she
wants.

However, for a woman to look nice *for her husband*
in order to please him is really an act of virtue! St.
Thomas Aquinas says that a woman "may use means
to please her husband." Therefore, looking nice for him
is really an act of charity, "lest through despising her,
he fall into adultery."[16] The Bible even says that the
woman "that is married thinketh on the things of the
world, *how she may please her husband.*" (*1 Corinthians* 7:34). So, married ladies, feel free to look attractive for your hubby!

The ugly flip side of this is when a woman wants to
look "sexy" for other men. Sorry, but that's not acceptable! Our Lord said, "Whosoever shall look on a woman
to lust after her, hath already committed adultery with
her in his heart." (*Matthew* 5:28). Since we all know
that adultery is a mortal sin, and even *one* mortal sin
unrepented when a person dies will send him to Hell
for eternity, then why do you think a woman would
want to tempt a man to lust after her by dressing in
a less than modest, dignified manner and be partially
responsible for his sin?[17] Especially if that sin could
condemn him? Women who dress this way probably
aren't thinking about—or may not even be aware of—
all the consequences of their clothing choices.

Here's an analogy that a friend gave me:

If we had a friend come to us and ask us to borrow

a gun so that she could kill someone, would we give our friend a gun? Of course not. To kill another human being is wrong, and we would not participate in that. Wouldn't you agree?

By the same token, we should not want to dress in a manner that would give a man the means to kill his own soul.[18] Shouldn't we, instead, take some preventative measures by dressing with modesty and dignity? Isn't a soul far more important than a body?

And shouldn't we feel embarrassed or humiliated to show too much of our bodies or our figures to the general public? Goodness, I can't remember the last time I heard someone say she was ashamed to be seen wearing a particular outfit because it was too revealing. Can you?

When my daughter was only six years old, she saw a young woman at the store wearing a very tight and revealing outfit. She shook her innocent little head and exclaimed, "Mommy! That girl doesn't like herself very much." Out of the mouths of babes!

People don't seem to be ashamed of anything they wear (or do!) anymore. Today's cavalier attitude toward "modesty"—and even "family honor"—really goes back to our lack of respect for ourselves, for God, and for His Law.

But keep in mind that even when a person is protected by grace and a life of prayer, many will still fall into the nets of indecency, impropriety and immodesty. Remember King David and Bathsheba? Gracious, if even David—the author of the *Psalms* and a chosen instrument of God—can make that big a mistake, then not one of us is immune!

But grace, prayer and a well-formed conscience will help us identify what is decent and honorable because we can't count on our society. Modern pop culture has lost any sense of what is proper, decent, respectable or modest. As C. S. Lewis said, when you are lost, retracing your steps to find your way back to the proper trail is actually progress. So let's look back in history to find out what respectability has always been and always meant.

Dr. Alice von Hildebrand pointed out to me that from the time that Adam and Eve were booted out of the Garden of Eden, it has been a sign of respectability and distinction to have clothing totally veiling our bodies—especially the female body.

Why?

Dr. von Hildebrand makes the point that anything that is precious, mysterious, and sacred is hidden from view. It is veiled.[19]

This reminds me of one of the things my grandmother told me when I was little: In nature, God made the valuable things difficult to get to. I heard the Reverend Billy Graham say that same thing once in a sermon. And even Muhammad Ali said the same thing to his daughter. But Ali went a bit further:

> Where do you find diamonds? Deep down in the ground, covered and protected. Where do you find pearls? Deep down at the bottom of the ocean, covered up and protected in a beautiful shell. Where do you find gold? Way down in the mine, covered over with layers and layers of rock. You've got to work hard to get to them . . . Your body is sacred. You're far more precious than diamonds and pearls, and you should be covered too.[20]

Yes, our bodies are much more precious than diamonds, pearls or gold! After all, through Baptism we are temples of the Holy Spirit. Shouldn't our precious bodies be veiled and hidden from view? St. Bernard of Clairvaux exclaimed, "How beautiful, then, is modesty, and what a gem among virtues it is."

We see veils being used as a sign of respect and sacredness in Scripture as well.

In the Old Testament Temple, the Holy of Holies was veiled. Only the Chief Priest was allowed to enter the Holy of Holies, and then only once a year! For here dwelt God's intimate presence between the wings of the two angels mounted on the Ark of the Covenant.

Even now, in these days of irreverence, things that are holy and sacred are still veiled.

In the Catholic Church, the Tabernacle is traditionally veiled.[21] How about the ciborium that holds the Blessed Sacrament? Traditionally, it always had a veil over it. Also, there is the canopy that is carried over the Blessed Sacrament in a procession. And how about the humeral veil that the priest wears draped over his shoulders, arms and hands during Benediction, so that even his consecrated hands do not touch the golden monstrance that contains Our Lord's Body?

All these "veilings" show respect and reverence for mystery and sacredness.

In addition to St. Paul's comments on veiling (*1 Corinthians* 11:15), Dr. Alice von Hildebrand pointed out to me another dimension of "the veil." Women, by their physical nature, are the very vessels of life. So *every* woman—due to the nature of her God-given femininity—has a certain mystery and sacredness, which is her ability to cooperate with her husband and with God in the sacredness of creation. How appropriate that a woman's awe-inspiring privilege is recognized by veiling! This is a deeply meaningful custom that has, unfortunately for women today, fallen by the wayside with many female church-goers.

Growing up, I remember seeing all the women wearing mantillas at Mass. I couldn't wait to be old enough so that I could wear one too! Alas, women and girls wearing veils are not a common sight anymore in most Catholic churches. But I have noticed more and more women have started to wear veils at Mass again.

Now that I understand that it is an honor for women

to be veiled, I think that the veil is a beautiful way of honoring the sacred calling and privilege of women.[22] Plus, it is a holy custom that was followed by all the female Saints of the Church.

What an honor we have as women to be given the glorious ability to carry another human life growing within our bodies. Think about it: Even though Eve carries a great portion of the responsibility for Original Sin, she is still given the glorious title: The Mother of all the Living.[23]

But it was the Blessed Virgin Mary who brought honor back to all women with her *Fiat*—"Be it done." She gave birth to the promised Redeemer, and we all benefit from the consent she gave to God's will when she said, "Be it done unto me according to thy word." (*Luke* 1:38). But women benefit most of all because Mary was proclaimed "blessed among women."[24]

We pay tribute to Mary daily with the *Hail Mary*, and all women now share in that honor by virtue of their womanhood and their dignified use of it. No wonder G. K. Chesterton wrote, "No one staring at that frightful female privilege can quite believe in the equality of the sexes . . ."[25]

Holy Scripture and Catholic devotions are full of fabulous examples of the marvelous role of women.[26] Many of the mysteries of the Rosary are directed at Mary. And how about the Stations of the Cross? "Jesus Meets His Sorrowful Mother," "Veronica Wipes the Face of Jesus," "The Women of Jerusalem Weep over Jesus." Almost all those assembled at the foot of the Cross are holy women. (The only Apostle who remained to the end was the young St. John.)

I have absolutely no intention to male-bash, but where were the other Apostles and the disciples during Our Lord's Passion?

"The first witness of the Resurrection was a woman— Mary Magdalen;" but even then, the men didn't believe her!²⁷ And in the *Apocalypse* (12:1), St. John saw a vision of a woman "clothed with the sun," crowned with stars.²⁸ The Church has traditionally interpreted this to be the Blessed Virgin Mary.

Women are actually granted an honorable position in the work of Redemption, and the Catholic Church "has elevated women to an extraordinary dignity."²⁹

Yes, yes, I know that women have been belittled over the course of human history. But "the culprits are always *individual* men."³⁰ The humiliation of women is not supported by the teachings of Christ or the Catholic Church.

In fact, in creating the first woman, God said, "Let us make him a help *like unto himself.*" (*Genesis* 2:18, emphasis added). *Like* Adam, not *inferior* to him. And St. Paul writes, "There is neither Jew nor Greek: there is neither bond nor free: *there is neither male nor female*, for you are all one in Christ Jesus." (*Galatians* 3:28, emphasis added).³¹

Also, the Church does not make any distinction between male and female in the administration of the Sacraments of Baptism, Confirmation, Penance, the Holy Eucharist, Matrimony and Extreme Unction— only in Holy Orders, which is reserved to men alone.

How about education? Historically, in secular cultures, only the men and boys were educated. But the Catholic Church has regularly founded schools to educate all Catholics . . . including women and girls.

Now here's a biggie: marriage!

At the time of Christ, divorce was common. It's easy to see what position a woman held in those times. She was pretty much a servant and a tool of man and often a plaything of his passions. The consent of a young woman was sometimes not even required in marriage. Her father gave her to whom he wished, or to whoever paid the most for her.

Among many pagan cultures, civil law gave the husband absolute power over his wife. He could punish her at will, sell her as a slave, or even put her to death.

In one of St. Jerome's letters (340-420), he speaks of a Roman woman who had been passed around to 23 different husbands. Twenty-three! It boggles the mind.

Even among the Jews, there was the so-called *bill of divorce*, by which a husband could put away his wife for any reason. Divorce was permitted by the authorities in Our Lord's time, as Jesus said, "Because Moses, by reason of the hardness of your heart, permitted you to put away your wives; but from the beginning it was not so." (*Matthew* 19:8). Nonetheless, Our Lord corrected this abuse of the Moral Law when He said, "But I say to you that whosoever shall put away his wife . . . maketh her to commit adultery; and he that shall marry her that is put away commits adultery." (*Matthew* 5:32).

However, Jesus Christ elevated marriage to a Sacrament. "A great Sacrament," St. Paul calls it. He compares the union of husband and wife to the union of Christ with the Church, His spouse. (*Ephesians* 5:22-23). Jesus restored the unity, indissolubility and sanctity of marriage and made the woman the queen in the marriage and of the home.

The Church calls this Sacrament "Matrimony." Look at the root meaning of this word: *Matri* and *munus* mean "the duty of motherhood." The word "matrimony" itself tells us the purpose of God in instituting marriage.[32] (There is also a hint of *"one"* ("mon") mother in a monogamous relationship, not two or three—or 23!)

St. Paul calls upon husbands to "love your wives, as Christ also loved the Church, and delivered himself up for it . . . Let every one of you in particular love his wife as himself." (*Ephesians* 5:25, 33).

I've told my husband that I have the easier part. I

only have to *obey* him. He has to *love* me (with all of my mood swings and fussiness) and be willing to take a bullet for me! His clout as head of the family comes with a price.

In marriage, the authority of the husband also has definite limits. Yes, he is the head of the family. But he is to exercise his authority for the welfare of his wife and children. Jesus Christ, the perfect example for all husbands, died for the Church. Husbands are called to have that same love for their families.

Are all husbands today willing to use their authority only for the welfare of the family? Are they willing to "go over Niagara Falls" to preserve the sanctity of their marriage?

Through the centuries, the Catholic Church has suffered strife, persecutions and injuries of every sort in order to preserve the sanctity of marriage as established by Christ.

As an example, consider King Henry VIII. In effect, he wanted a divorce. Actually, he wanted his valid marriage to Catherine of Aragon to be declared invalid (he wanted an illegitimate annulment). Henry was threatening either divorce or schism! Pope Clement VII answered that Henry was married to his wife Catherine until death!

To preserve the sanctity and indissolubility of marriage, the Pope permitted an entire nation to break away from the Church, rather than tamper with Our Lord's command: "What therefore God hath joined together, let no man put asunder." (*Matthew* 19:6). Actually, the Pope had no other choice, in obedience to Christ.

Our present legislators should hear this story! We must preserve the sanctity, dignity and unity of marriage, the sacred union which God established for the procreation and raising of children. For once divorce becomes widespread, a society begins to fall apart—

which we can all see happening right here in our own country.

Preserving the dignity of marriage also preserves the dignity of women, since women are physically made to be mothers.

So much of reproduction is mysteriously related to women because it is in the female body that a new life will be created and from which it will be born.

The Church hasn't officially declared *exactly* when God places a soul into an unborn baby's body. But from our current scientific knowledge, we know that the "blueprint" of the entire person is present in the DNA at the moment of fertilization—when sperm meets egg. So we can assume that it is at that moment (fertilization) that God "reaches down" and places the soul into the newly conceived child within the woman's body. So, as Dr. Alice von Hildebrand points out, a mother will during her pregnancy carry two souls within her body—her own and that of her unborn child.[33]

The relationship between God and the woman—who carries within her this new human being from the very moment of fertilization—is mysterious, glorious, awe-inspiring and deserving of reverence. Since it is inside the female body that God implants the soul of the new human being,[34] the female body is like a sanctuary— a shelter or safe haven—and you certainly can't say that about the male body.

G. K. Chesteron wrote, "Nothing can ever overcome that one enormous sex [female] superiority, that even the male child is born closer to his mother than to his father."[35] Childbirth itself is shrouded in a certain sacredness.[36] Dr. Alice von Hildebrand wrote the following:

> Granted that the agonizing pains that many women
> endure are a dire consequence of Original Sin, the
> beauty of Catholic teaching makes it clear that her

> womanly travails and cries of agony, which precede
> the coming into the world of another human person,
> have a deeply symbolic meaning. Just as Christ has
> suffered the agonizing pains of the crucifixion in
> order to reopen for us the gates of Heaven, so the
> woman has received the costly privilege of suffering
> so that another child, made to God's image and like-
> ness, can enter into the world.[37]

Wow! When you put it that way, it certainly gives
labor and delivery a whole new meaning.

Not only that, but every single child a woman has
conceived will live forever. Each and every new-born
infant has an immortal soul made to the image and
likeness of God. (*Genesis* 1:26). Think about that for a
moment. It's awe-inspiring.

The sacredness and mystery of a woman's God-given
femininity is an awesome privilege! Now, consider the
case of a scantily clad woman who doesn't mind being
ogled and lusted after by any man who happens to
cross her path. This takes on a whole new perspective,
doesn't it?

What do women's fashions have to do with loss of
respect for femininity? Dr. Alice von Hildebrand has
written:

> The fearful sexual decadence that we have wit-
> nessed in the course of the last forty years can be
> traced back, at least in part, to the fashion world's
> systematic attempt to eradicate in girls the "holy
> bashfulness" which is the proper response that women
> should give to what is personal, intimate, and calls
> for veiling. To dress modestly is the appropriate
> response that women should give to their "mystery."
> *Noblesse oblige.*[38]
>
> The fashions of the day are all geared toward
> destroying women's sensitivity for the dignity of their
> sex. Deep sadness is called for when one watches
> Western girls running around practically naked and

then compares them with how the Hindu and Moslem women are clothed with modesty, grace, and dignity. No doubt, a mastermind has initiated these decadent fashions which aim at destroying female modesty.[39]

Yes, the proper response that women should give to what is personal, intimate and calls for "veiling" is to dress with modesty and dignity. But the fashions of today seem pretty well geared toward destroying our understanding of the dignity of womanhood.

It hasn't always been this way. What have fashions been like since the time of Adam and Eve?

NOTES

1. D. Q. McInerny, *Philosophical Psychology* (Elmhurst, PA: The Priestly Fraternity of St. Peter, 1999), p. 182-183, 203.
2. D. Q. McInerny, *A Course in Thomistic Ethics* (Elmhurst, PA: The Priestly Fraternity of St. Peter, 1997), p. 94.
3. *Ibid.*, pp. 116-117.
4. McInerny, *Philosophical Psychology*, p. 182.
5. *Ibid.*, p. 203.
6. *Ibid.,* p. 206.
7. Patricia Pitkus Bainbridge, M.A., "It's No Big Deal . . . Or Is It?" in *Life Matters* (Rockford, IL: Respect Life Office of the Diocese of Rockford), Vol. III, no. 12, Sept. 2004.
8. Fr. Regis Scanlon, O.F.M., *Homiletic and Pastoral Review*, Nov. 1988, quoted in Bainbridge, *op. cit.*
9. *Genesis ad lit.*, xi, 30.
10. According to the Baltimore Catechism, "Grace is a supernatural gift of God bestowed on us through the merits of Jesus Christ for our salvation." (No. 109). "Sanctifying Grace is that grace which confers on our souls a new life, that is, a sharing in the life of God Himself." (No. 111). Sanctifying Grace "makes us holy and pleasing to God." (No. 112). Baptism and Confession give (or restore) Sanctifying Grace, and the other Sacraments increase Sanctifying Grace in our soul. (*St. Joseph Baltimore Catechism*, Official Revised Edition, No. 2, explained by Rev. Bennet Kelley, C.P., Catholic Book Publishing Co., NY, 1962).

11. *Civitate Dei,* xiii, 13.
12. Alice von Hildebrand, *op. cit.,* pp. 24-25.
13. *Ibid.,* p. 36.
14. Alice von Hildebrand, *op. cit.,* p. 23.
15. http://www.priestsforlife.org/brochures/mtspeech.html
16. *Summa Theologica,* II-II, Q. 169, art. 2. From the edition translated by Fathers of the English Dominican Province, Benziger Bros., New York, 1948.
17. Cf. Tracy Tucciarone Lopez, "Modesty," www.kensmen.com/catholic/modesty.html
18. Using the word "kill" in reference to a soul is accurate in that a mortal sin drives the Divine Life, Sanctifying Grace, from the soul. However, the human soul does not die (lose its human life) when the person commits a mortal sin.
19. Alice von Hildebrand, *op. cit.,* p. 83.
20. Hana Yasmeen Ali, *More Than a Hero: Muhammad Ali's Life Lessons Presented through His Daughter's Eyes,* Pocket Books, 2000.
21. Alice von Hildebrand, *op. cit.,* p. 83.
22. *Ibid.,* p. 89.
23. *Ibid.,* pp. 16, 61.
24. Msgr. Luigi Civardi, *How Christ Changed the World: The Social Principles of the Catholic Church,* 1961; TAN, 1991, p. 5.
25. G. K. Chesterton, *What's Wrong with the World* (New York: Sheed and Ward, 1956), p. 192, in von Hildebrand, *op. cit.,* p. 87.
26. Alice von Hildebrand, *op. cit.,* pp. 17-18.
27. *Ibid.,* p. 18.
28. *Ibid.,* p. 19.
29. *Ibid.,* pp. 19, 20.
30. *Ibid.,* p. 20.
31. This paragraph and the following paragraphs regarding women in Church history are largely taken from Civardi, *op. cit.,* pp. 3-6.
32. Canon Francis Ripley, *This Is The Faith* (1951; Third Edition, TAN, 2002), p. 338.
33. Cf. Alice von Hildebrand, *op. cit.,* pp. 63, 86.
34. *Ibid.*
35. Chesterton, *op. cit.,* Chapter I, p. 3 PP., in von Hildebrand, *op. cit.,* p. 87.
36. Alice von Hildebrand, *op. cit.,* p. 87.
37. *Ibid.*
38. *Noblesse oblige* means "Nobility obligates"; i.e., those who hold an honorable position have a duty to behave in an honorable manner.
39. Alice von Hildebrand, *op. cit.,* pp. 89-90.

CHAPTER THREE

Corruption of Fashions

"And the eyes of them both were opened: and when
they perceived themselves to be naked, they sewed
together fig leaves, and made themselves aprons. . . .
    And the Lord God made for Adam and his wife,
garments of skins, and clothed them." —*Genesis* 3:7, 21

EVIDENTLY, the "aprons" that Adam and Eve
made for themselves didn't provide enough
coverage in God's eyes, so He made them garments of skins and dressed them properly.

Have you ever wondered what those skin garments
looked like? You can bet they weren't those skimpy
"Tarzan-and-Jane" outfits seen in the movies.

In the verses from *Genesis* cited above, the Latin
Vulgate uses the word *tunicas*. Even for someone not
well versed in Latin, I think it's obvious that that word
means "tunic." The Hebrew word used is *ktnvt*, the root
of which means "cover."[1]

Tunics of pre-Christian biblical and ancient Roman
times were flowing garments that extended past the
knees and covered the arms and shoulders. I feel
pretty confident that, after that whole embarrassing
issue in the Garden with the Serpent, Adam and Eve
made sure their children and grandchildren all dressed
modestly.

Adam and Eve lived long enough to see many generations of their children grow up and have children
of their own. Scripture tells us that Adam died shortly
before Noah was born. Imagine Adam and Eve's grief

at having to watch their children grow up, knowing that, because of their sin, their children would never experience anything like Adam and Eve had in the Garden of Eden. Right down to today, children often have to suffer because of the sins and mistakes of their parents.

I think that another outcome from that incident in Paradise is that women have an inordinate interest in clothing. Yes, we can't deny it! I can just imagine women in Moses' day gossiping about what the other women were wearing. Not only that: simply consider how much and how often women's fashions change compared to men's. But that doesn't mean that men don't have their own frivolous pastimes. Look at how many men have gotten overly involved in competition and sports, sometimes to the exclusion of everything else.

ESPN. Need I say more?

I think it's because of women's interest in clothing that we even have a record to trace. There are historians who have kept track of this stuff! Let's take a look.

From the time of Adam and Eve, men and women have dressed with dignity. Straight through the era of Noah, Abraham, Isaac, Jacob, Moses and King David, women all wore long, flowing, graceful "tunics" that covered their shoulders and usually their arms and extended to the ground, and they would wear some sort of veil to cover their heads.

Early pagan Greek women wore long flowing robes and gowns, with their heads covered with some sort of veil or hair ornament. The garment was called a *chiton* (begins with a "k" sound and rhymes with "tighten"). The basic male garment was also the chiton, but it was usually only knee-length. The chiton was made of a rectangle of fabric which was fastened at the shoulders and belted at the waist. The garment could be either sleeved or sleeveless. Both styles were very graceful.

In Rome, the women wore a floor-length sleeveless tunic (men wore a knee-length tunic), over which they wore a floor-length *stola*, which was a tunic-type garment with sleeves. It was belted at the waist, and in public they would finish off their outfit with an elegant veil.

Basic styles in the Christian West didn't change much for centuries. From the historically accepted "Fall of Rome" in 476 A.D. until the time of the Crusades, the wealthier women wore elegant gowns that reached the floor, complete with long sleeves and often a veil, especially for married women. Marriage often meant a change in hair style too: from loose and flowing to pinned up in some type of a bun. Women would sometimes wear two tunic-type garments, one over the other.

The veil was worn over a wimple, a piece of white fabric which covered the head and neck and sometimes even the chin. Cloistered nuns still wear a wimple (as in photos of St. Therese of Lisieux.) The Collettine Poor Clares simplified their wimple in the early 20th century so that it no longer covers their chin.

A "girdle," which was a belt or sash worn over the tunic, was gracefully wrapped around the waist or over the hips.

It wasn't until the late 1500's that fashions became more ornate, although the basic clothing remained the same: long gowns, long sleeves, with some sort of head-covering. Think of "Elizabethan England," with the ruffle around the neck and large "leg-of-mutton" sleeves, and you'll get a good idea of what they were wearing during that time period. Lots of attractive embroidery and beautiful decoration were also included on the clothing. Instead of wimples, women wore fancy head-dresses of various styles, sometimes with a veil attached to the back.

Around this time, the corset was introduced. This was a stiff undergarment that shaped the bodice and narrowed the waist. The corset would become one of the classic elements of women's clothing. In some fashion eras, it was used in order to achieve a *very* tiny waist size.

A "fashion revolution" took place around the time of the French Revolution (1789-1804) and Napoleon Bonaparte (1804-1815), with Napoleon's wife Josephine setting a trend of high-waisted dresses with straight, boyish silhouettes and flattened bust lines. This is also the "Jane Austen" look, as seen in movies like *Pride and Prejudice* and *Sense and Sensibility*: high waist, low-cut bodice, long straight skirt, long narrow sleeves or short puffy sleeves or a combination of both. Also notable in women's clothing at this time period were more masculine trimmings and accessories, such as top hats instead of bonnets, and military braid on their garments. This "fashion revolution" didn't last long, as women's fashions soon returned to their traditional styles.

In the young United States of America at this time, waistlines were usually at the natural waistline and styles were fancy. Men were wearing ruffled shirts, tight knee-breeches and powdered wigs, as seen in portraits of George Washington.

In the mid-1800's, skirts became *very* full, with hoops and crinoline petticoats underneath. Photos of ladies during the Civil War show this style. Men were wearing top hats. Then came the bustle at the back of the dress. A few years later, before and after the year 1900, the styles featured wide shoulders with large (sometimes enormous) sleeves, and tiny waists. (There's the corset again!)

Incidentally, in all of this discussion about fashions, we're talking about what is worn by *good* women, which has historically meant women who are *chaste*, whether married or unmarried.

On the other hand, women who are making a living

by living an openly unchaste life have historically worn clothing that is intentionally immodest and sexually provocative.

At the beginning of the 1900's, the styles start to look a little more familiar to us, a little more "modern." Hemlines move up a few inches above the ankle, and fashions are overall simpler than before.

You'll notice that one theme has remained constant in women's fashions during the six thousand years of human history: Women wore loose, flowing, feminine gowns that reached the floor, usually with long sleeves and some sort of head covering or hair ornament. But fashions were about to change radically, and not just in the amount of fullness or the length of the skirt. So what happened?

Women's clothing trends followed roughly the same pattern as the trends in society (and helped to shape those trends.) Social scientists point to the Industrial Revolution (starting roughly around 1800)—which enabled women to work outside the home. Then in the year 1920, the 19th Amendment to the Constitution was passed, giving women the right to vote.

The Roaring Twenties were the period when we start to see a *dramatic* departure from the classic style of dressing!

Short hair and the boyish silhouette of the flapper look, with skirts raised to the knees and sleeveless bodices, emerged for women.[2] But where did those unprecedented styles and ideas come from? Certainly not from the past few thousand years of human history.

Yes, the times were changing—but one particular woman pushed them to change faster.

Gabrielle Bonheur Chanel, who would become famous under the name of Coco Chanel, played a very important role in the change of women's fashions. It has been said that she *revolutionized* women's fashions. By the way, the perfume "Chanel No. 5" was named after Coco Chanel.

Coco Chanel's personal life was tragic, beginning with the death of her mother and abandonment by her father by the time she was 12. At 17, she moved to an orphanage run by nuns. Later, she picked up her nickname when she went through a short career as a dancer, actress and cabaret singer. Her affair with a wealthy man financed her first hat business, located in Paris.

Another boyfriend, Arthur ("Boy") Capel, financed her expansion from hats to clothing. Her early fashions were women's clothing made out of wool jersey (stretchy knit fabric, not woven)—which had been used only for men's underwear—and she used it to make clingy dresses. Those sexy, clingy styles brought her the beginning of her success. Coco would also make outfits for herself out of men's sport coats and ties.

During World War I (1914-1918), the German occupation of Northern France meant the fashion business in Paris was cut off for some years. But shortly after the Great War, Chanel was back in business.

By the 1920's, Chanel's fashion house had expanded considerably, and her short, straight dress set a fashion trend with its "little boy" look.

One evening, Coco accidentally scorched her hair with a curling iron before going to the Paris Opera. She cut her hair very short and went to the opera anyway. Her short hair style, known as "bobbed" hair, became a trend.

About that same time, designers Yves Saint-Laurent and Courreges introduced dressy pantsuits for women.[3] However, nearly all women rejected the idea of wearing pants, and designers didn't try that again until much later.

As mentioned, Coco Chanel was very influential on the fashion scene. In addition to the bobbed hairstyle and the unisex style of dressing, she introduced the "little black dress," the use of clingy knits, slacks (in her own wardrobe) and women's bathing suits.

Wait . . . bathing suits?

That's right.

The ancient Greeks and Romans practiced "bathing" (swimming) in bath houses. These places became recreational centers where men would also meet, discuss current events, etc. Bathing for men and women was separate, and mixed bathing was even condemned by Emperors Hadrian and Marcus Aurelius, and in the Eastern Roman Empire by Justinian I.[4] Some may say that it was different in Ancient Rome since people swam in the nude—but have you been to the beach lately? What I've seen some women wearing isn't that far from nudity!

Separate bath houses for men and women continued in one form or another through the centuries. By the 1400's, mixed swimming occurred in some establishments, and these places were known for their promiscuity. Mixed bath houses were considerd hotbeds of vice, as only women with loose morals would swim in mixed company. Actually, the word "stew" originally meant bath house but came to be another name for a brothel.[5]

Over the centuries, respectable bath houses continued to be separate. Before the mid-18th century, mixed swimming was condemned by Catholics, Protestants, Jews and Muslims as an occasion for vice.[6] From the latter half of the 1800's, women who went bathing—usually outdoors—wore an elaborate bathing outfit which included sleeves, a skirt, and loose pantaloons to below the knee. The fabric used was basically the same heavy fabric used in other clothing—so today we would hardly even consider such an outfit a "real" bathing suit.

But Coco Chanel introduced a bathing suit made out of lightweight, clingy jersey; it still had long sleeves, extended past the knees, and was covered by a long skirt. This sounds like plenty of coverage to us now, but back then the suit caused quite a stir . . . and a fair share of scandal.

In 1931, movie mogul Samuel Goldwin hired Chanel as fashion manager for the stars. However, the divas of the day apparently did not like Chanel's unglamorous clothing. Also, filmgoers wanted to escape the Depression by watching movies that featured stars wearing beautiful clothing.

Due to her affair with a German officer, Chanel fell out of favor. She spent 15 years in Switzerland in exile.

During World War II (1939-1945), women in the U.S. worked in factories, where they would wear trousers and coveralls. But outside of the workplace, women kept their feminine style of dressing.

In 1946, a bomb was dropped in the fashion world. It was called the *bikini*. I always wondered where the name "bikini" came from, and amazingly enough, I found out through an article written in 1997 by Steve Rushin in *Sports Illustrated*.

Rushin relates that Louis Réard, a French automotive engineer who was running his mother's lingerie business, named his new two-piece, "atom-sized" swimsuit after the testing site of the atomic bomb in the Pacific Ocean: Bikini Atoll. Since the bikini was so tiny, none of the models in Paris would wear it on the fashion runways. So, according to Rushin, Réard hired Micheline Bernardini, whose regular job was as a nude dancer at the Casino de Paris. She "had no qualms" about strolling down the runway in this bathing suit.[7]

Rushin continues:

> The world took notice. In Catholic countries— Spain, Portugal, and Italy—The bikini was banned. Decency leagues pressured Hollywood to keep it out of the movies. One writer said it's a "two piece bathing suit which reveals everything about a girl except for her mother's maiden name."[8]

At first, the bikini was rejected in the U.S. by the "prudish Americans," and a 1954 issue of *Vogue* magazine featured a swimsuit with matching jacket as "still another way of looking dressed, not undressed."[9]

"As recently as 1957, *Modern Girl* magazine sniffed, 'It is hardly necessary to waste words over the so-called bikini, since it is inconceivable that any girl with tact and decency would ever wear such a thing.'"[10]

Other bikini "landmarks" in the U.S. would be the song "Itsy Bitsy Teenie Weenie Yellow Polka Dot Bikini," which came out in 1960, and the movie *Beach Party*, starring Annette Funicello and Frankie Avalon (1963). This movie, which was followed by several sequels, featured young women dancing in bikinis on screen.

Interestingly, Annette Funicello herself refused to wear a bikini in any of her movies, though she occasionally wore a two-piece suit.[11] Her fellow actress, Donna Loren, also refused, saying, "I don't believe in going up there, sticking a bikini on and shaking around."[12]

Annette's refusal was included in her contract at the request of Walt Disney.[13] But unfortunately, few women in the acting business followed her example.

Thankfully, it seems the "tankini" is moving back to a somewhat more covered-up look in women's bathing suits. But maybe we need to rethink the whole concept of publicly showing off our bodies!

It was about the same time as the bikini appeared in 1946 that Christian Dior introduced longer, flared skirts and belted waists. These defined shapes brought back the more feminine form to dressing . . . as well as undergarments that helped the "not so perfect" body to fit into these new fashion shapes! This decade saw the introduction of the "bullet bra" and the "push-up" bra.

In 1954, Chanel decided to re-enter the fashion world by revamping and reintroducing her designs from the

1930's. Some say that Chanel's comeback was a reaction to Dior's feminine styles.

When Coco Chanel returned, her popularity skyrocketed. She introduced bell-bottom pants for women, which were not popular, but which planted the seed for women to start wearing slacks.

Suddenly, the Hollywood stars loved Coco's fashions, and her designs were worn by Anne Baxter, Elizabeth Taylor and Audrey Hepburn.

The 1960's were a time of great changes in society. Fashions moved away from reflecting the traditional female role and away from voluptuous figures, like those of Marilyn Monroe and Jayne Mansfield in the 1950's.[14] Due to Chanel, the fashion world's attention shifted once again to a straight, boyish shape. Think of the sudden popularity of British model Twiggy during the 1960's.[15]

"Jacqueline Kennedy's tea suit and pillbox hat" was a brief rage in the early 1960's, but "before long, sex was the buzzword and the megawatt spotlight focused on youth. Skirts shot up. Pantyhose appeared. The world said goodbye to the girdle."[16]

That was the period when the Annette Funicello and Frankie Avalon beach-party movies came out. Coincidentally, it was in 1963 that radical feminist Gloria Steinem published *A Bunny's Tale* and *The Beach Book*.

What a crazy time period the 1960's were, with their neon colors and modern art! Looking back, I can hardly believe the culture embraced those styles that, to me now, are so ugly. Many women wore clothing they didn't like because they couldn't find anything else. Sound familiar?

One of the big changes of the 1970's was the shift toward women working outside the home.[17] At that time Gloria Steinem began lecturing on the feminist circuit, founded *Ms. Magazine* and became politically involved. But as G. K. Chesterton had written nearly

50 years earlier, "a feminist is someone who loathes being a woman and who dislikes the chief feminine characteristics."[18] Like Steinem, Chesterton freely acknowledged that women had been wronged in the past. Chesterton's solution was to "destroy the tyranny." But, he was quick to point out, the feminists "want to destroy the womanhood."[19]

Before long, designers were showing slacks on the runways. Then came designer jeans. "Jeans became the symbol of revolution." Remember Brooke Shields and her Calvin Kleins? This symbol of the feminist movement was clearly something different from what women of refinement had always worn.[20]

Before long, pants became common attire for women and girls for school, work and even church. It was also in the 1960's and 1970's that the birth control pill began to gain acceptance even among many Catholics.

Advertising agencies quickly prepared marketing research to find out the reaction of men to a woman wearing pants. Do you know what they found? Using newly developed technology, they tracked the path that a man's eyes take when looking at a woman in pants. They found that when a man looked at a woman in pants from the back, he looked directly at her bottom. When he looked at a woman wearing pants from the front, advertisers found that his eyes dropped directly to a woman's most private and intimate area. Not her face! Not her chest!

Advertisers figured out a long time ago how to apply Gestalt psychology and the Law of Closure[21] and the Law of Good Continuation[22] when devising advertising that is aimed at men. Gracious, what does all of that mean?

It means that the eye will follow a line, and a viewer will complete the picture with his or her imagination. Think of the little AOL logo man. A stick figure, right? But we all know what he's doing.

Advertisers know that the same holds true when a man views a woman wearing slacks or a skirt with slits. Men's eyes will follow the lines right up her legs and finish the picture in their imagination. Women's eyes may do the same thing, but since women don't have the same type of temptations, their imaginations don't complete the picture in the same way as men's do.

I have received letters and emails from men who had read the first edition of this book and wanted me to tell women that they didn't need that marketing study to tell them what they already knew: When a woman is wearing pants, a man's eyes will (much to his embarrassment) fall to a woman's crotch. These men also pointed out that it is something that happens without their wanting to do it, or without their realizing it. It's the nature of men "to look" . . . *and they do!* By the way, you'll notice that, in ads, models in trousers will sit with their legs far apart. This isn't being done by accident.

The 1970's saw a brief popularity for ankle-length skirts, but this style was basically rejected.[23] Take note! *The women of the 1970's rejected current fashions. Today we can reject current fashions as well!*

The 1980's continued to move toward more casual attire, and they are remembered as the decade of huge shoulder pads, huge earrings and huge hair styles.

In the 1990's a new term was coined to reflect the new casual (some would say "sloppy") style of dress in the workplace: "business casual."[24]

Some people have claimed that the pendulum has gone so far to one side in fashions that now it's going to fly back. Then, they claim, things are going to be fine. *I* used to think that as well—until Dr. Alice von Hildebrand pointed out to me that it's not a matter of a pendulum swinging. It's about rising above a debased culture.

Our culture is wallowing in confusion and moral darkness, with "the blind leading the blind!" People of true Christian faith today must rise above all of the errors and sensuality. We must elevate ourselves to a higher level of life and culture by dressing with dignity.

Think about it! Even prostitutes in the 1950's and 1960's did not wear the skimpy, suggestive clothing that many women and young girls are now wearing to the shopping malls during warm weather.

What has happened to change our culture these past 100 years? Was it cultural, political . . . or even something demonic?

NOTES

1. "Modesty," www.kensmen.com/catholic/modesty
2. "Dressing for a New Millenium," *The Holland Sentinel*, January 3, 2000.
   www.thehollandsentinel.net/stories/010300/fea_dressing.html
3. *Ibid.*
4. *Encyclopedia Americana,* Vol. 3 (Danbury, CT: Grolier, Inc., 2000), p. 349.
5. *Ibid.*, p. 350.
6. *Ibid.*
7. Steve Rushin, "Bikini Waxing," *Sports Illustrated*, 1997.
   www.bikiniatoll.com/Bikiniwaxing.html#anchor456238
8. *Ibid.*
9. Emily Mitchell, "The Bikini Turns 50," *TIME International*, July 1, 1996. www.time.com/time/international/1996/960701/fashion
10. Rushin, *op. cit.*
11. Stephen J. McParland, Excerpt from "It's Party Time: A Musical Appreciation of the Beach Party Film Genre."
    www.encore4.net/livelyset/closeup/beach-party/beach2
12. *Ibid.*
13. *Ibid.*
14. *The Holland Sentinel, op. cit.*
15. *Ibid.*
16. *Ibid.*
17. *Ibid.*

18. G. K. Chesterton, *op. cit.*, p. 197, in von Hildebrand, *op. cit.*, p. 2.
19. Chesterton, *op. cit.*, p. 148, in von Hildebrand, *op. cit.*, p. 8.
20. *The Holland Sentinel, op. cit.*
21. The Law of Closure: "Humans tend to enclose a space by completing a contour and ignoring gaps in the figure." http://iit.ches.ua.edu/systems/gestalt.html
22. The Law of Good Continuation: "Humans tend to continue contours whenever the elements of the pattern establish an implied direction." *Ibid.*
23. *The Holland Sentinel, op. cit.*
24. *Ibid.*

CHAPTER FOUR

Designs against Modesty —and Catholic Response

". . . 'in order to destroy Catholicism, it is necessary
to commence by suppressing woman.' . . . but since we
cannot suppress woman, let us corrupt her . . ."
—Letter between two leading Freemasons,
dated August 9, 1838 (cf. p. 56 below)

"Religion does not fear the dagger's point; but it can
vanish under corruption. Let us not grow tired
of corruption: we may use a pretext, such as sport, hygiene,
health resorts. It is necessary to corrupt,
that our boys and girls practice nudism in dress.
To avoid too much reaction, one would have to
progress in a methodical manner:
first, undress up to the elbow; then up to the knees;
then arms and legs completely uncovered; later, the
upper part of the chest, the shoulders, etc. etc."
—*International Review
on Freemasonry*, 1928

WHEN you look around at society today, you
can't help but notice the disintegration in
morals and values. And we know things don't
just happen by accident, so it would not be reasonable
to think that clothing styles went down the tube this
far and this fast just by chance.

Most of us have heard that Satan's biggest decep-
tion is convincing people that he doesn't exist. He has

been extremely busy, especially since the 1800's, working behind the scenes to oppose all that is beautiful, sacred and holy. One of the human groups he has used for this opposition has been Freemasonry (also known simply as Masonry).

When, how and why did the Freemasons begin their assault on women and fashions? In order to understand that, we have to dig back in history a bit. Stick with this chapter. You'll be glad you did.

In the late 1700's, Catholics found themselves fighting off the heresies of Jansenism, Quietism and Gallicanism. Jansenists held, among other errors, that it was impossible to keep some of God's commandments. Jansenism spread an atmosphere of harshness in matters of spirituality. Quietists held that the soul should be totally passive under the action of God and should not even make efforts to resist temptations. Gallicanists resisted papal authority in various ways.

When the French Revolution broke out in 1789 in France, priests and nuns were executed, churches and convents were closed, and for a while it was even a crime to attend Mass. Catholicism in France was replaced by the rule of "reason"—fostered by the Illuminati and Freemasonry[1]—which rapidly spread throughout the Western world. Nearly all of the countries of that area violated and blocked the rights of the Catholic Church in some way. The devil's plan was succeeding beautifully!

The Illuminati, a secret society within the Masonic lodges, of course rejected Catholic teaching and Divine Revelation. New members of the Illuminati were taught Rationalism: i.e., to believe only humanly discovered facts about life, human nature and the observable world. If they couldn't understand it through known science, they didn't believe it.

Those involved in the Illuminati were taught bitter anti-Catholicism. The *Encyclopedia* became the bible of the Enlightenment, Freemasonry provided the rituals and hierarchy, with the Catholic Church being the enemy.

In 1738, Pope Clement XII issued his papal bull *In Eminenti,* condemning Freemasonry and giving many reasons, including Freemasonry's "oaths of secrecy and of fidelity to Masonry."[2] He severely forbade Catholics to join Masonic societies, threatening an excommunication against those who would even "favor" these societies.[3]

In 1825, Pope Leo XII lamented the fact that governments had not paid attention to papal decrees against Masonry, and that thus Masonry had spawned even more dangerous sects.[4]

Pope Pius VIII wrote about the Masons in his Encyclical *Traditi* (1829): "Their law is untruth, their god is the devil, and their cult is turpitude."[5]

Pope Gregory XVI wrote in *Mirari Vos* (1832): "Evil comes out of secret societies, bottomless abyss of misery, which those conspiring societies have dug and in which heresies and sects have, as may be said, vomited as in a privy all they hold of licentiousness, sacrilege and blasphemy."[6]

Later, in *Humanum Genus* (1884), Pope Leo XIII would state that some Freemasons "have plainly determined and proposed that, artfully and of set purpose, the multitude should be satiated with a boundless license of vice, as when this had been done, it would easily come under their power and authority for any acts of daring."[7]

In fact, the Catholic Church has been so adamant in its stand against Freemasonry that Canon 1374 of the new *Code of Canon Law* (1983) stipulates: "One who joins an association which plots against the Church is to be punished with a just penalty; one who promotes or moderates such an association, however, is to be punished with an interdict."[8] The Vatican then reaffirmed that "The faithful who belong to Masonic associations are in a state of grave sin and may not receive Holy Communion."[9]

But let's get back to the early 1800's.

The "Illuminated Masons" were very outspoken in their desire to destroy the Catholic Church. Their goal was to destroy Christianity,[10] but they admitted that it couldn't be ruined from the outside. They had to make a two-pronged attack.

The founder of the Illuminati, Adam Weishaupt, had formulated one part of the strategy late in the 1700's: "We will infiltrate that place [*the Vatican*], and once inside, we will never come out. We will bore from within until nothing remains but an empty shell."[11]

The Masons aimed to infiltrate "the sacristies, the seminaries and the monasteries."[12] But it would take time for the Masons to get into Catholic institutions.[13] So they had another plan. It had to do with women.

". . . 'in order to destroy Catholicism, it is necessary to commence by suppressing woman. . . . But since we cannot suppress woman, let us corrupt her with the Church . . .'"[14]

Freemasons apparently understood that women are the moral compasses of society. The serpent knew this and approached Eve. Even Confucius said that woman is the moral root of society, and the culture will only grow in proportion to the moral strength of its women.[15]

Just as the Freemasons wanted to infiltrate the religious orders, they also planned to infiltrate the fashion world. They planned to influence women's and children's fashion trends and styles by getting their own people involved in the fashion industry. It was also the Illuminati's plan to form and control public opinion through the media.[16]

Around this time, St. John Bosco (1815-1888), who lived in Turin, Italy, was also fighting various worldly forces. The Saint received many visions in the form of dreams. The main thread of nearly all those dreams was the importance of maintaining innocence and purity.

The Catholic Church has always taught that all acts of impurity are *grave sins*—ALL OF THEM! Every impure thought or impure deed is a mortal sin (as long as the person realizes it is a grave matter and does it anyway).[17] The unfortunate reality is that today, these grave sins are sugar-coated and now encouraged as innocent (and even "healthy"!) "fantasizing." Just imagine what St. John Bosco would think if he could flip on a television today or walk into a shopping mall during warm weather!

Bl. Pope Pius IX (1846-1878) was the visible head of the Catholic Church during this time, and he spent most of his pontificate protecting Catholics by fighting numerous heresies. In his Encyclical *Quanta Cura* in 1864, he condemned sixteen popular but erroneous ideas. Along with this Encyclical he issued his famous *Syllabus Errorum—The Syllabus of Errors* (1864), which was a list of eighty condemned religious errors. *The Syllabus* created tremendous waves when published and has been outraging Liberals and Modernists ever since.

After condemning Freemasonry numerous times in several writings, Bl. Pius IX died in 1878 after serving 34 years, the longest pontificate in Church history.

Pope Leo XIII was then elected. Six years into his pontificate, on October 13, 1884—exactly 33 years to the day before the great Miracle of the Sun would take place in Fatima on October 13, 1917—Pope Leo XIII had an amazing vision. If anyone still doubts that Satan is working overtime to snatch souls from God, the vision of Pope Leo XIII should remove any uncertainty about the seriousness of our situation.

After offering Mass at the Vatican on October 13, 1884, Pope Leo XIII suffered some sort of a collapse and seemed unconscious for a brief period. When he came to, he exclaimed to those around him, "What a horrible picture I was permitted to see!" The Pope explained that he had seen the destruction to be worked by Satan in the coming years—approximately the period of the 20th century.

Another version of this account states that Pope Leo heard a conversation between Our Lord and Satan which went like this: Satan boasted, "I can destroy Your Church" if granted a certain period of time. Our Lord replied, "How long?" and Satan responded, "75 to 100 years."[18] Our Lord then agreed to let Satan have this period of greater freedom.[19]

As a result of this vision, Pope Leo XIII prescribed the Prayer to St. Michael the Archangel to be prayed by priest and people at the end of every Low Mass throughout the world.[20] Our family still prays it.

We may never know the precise details of Pope Leo's vision, but it surely seems that his concern about the coming difficulties in the Church and the world were well founded.

Pope Leo XIII, like many Popes before him, spoke out strongly against Freemasonry, Socialism and Communism. His wording in the encyclical *Rerum novarum* (May 15, 1891) is particularly strong, and his encyclical letter *Humanum Genus—On Freemasonry* (1884) is the greatest papal condemnation of Freemasonry.

Leo XIII died in 1903, which opened the door for another conclave. And something frightening almost happened.

Cardinal Mariano Rampolla entered the conclave favored to be the next Pope. But when it was discovered that he had a close affinity with the French Freemasons,[21] Emperor Franz Joseph of Austria used his traditional prerogative as Holy Roman Emperor to veto Cardinal Rampolla's candidacy.[22]

In further rounds of voting, the papacy was offered

to Giuseppe Melchiorre Sarto, whom we now know as Pope St. Pius X (1903-1914).

Pope St. Pius X understood the agenda of Freemasonry, as well as its ties to the Communist threat, and he knew well Leo XIII's encyclical *Rerum Novarum*. His goal was to educate the faithful about the errors of Modernism, Communism and false Nationalism. In that way, he felt he could prevent these errors from further infiltrating the Church and harming Catholics.

Even though influential people in society were saying that the Catholic Church was "out of touch" and "needed to modernize" in order to relate to the current culture and society, Pope St. Pius X wouldn't negotiate with the advocates of modern culture and contemporary philosophies.

Instead, he issued a decree entitled *Lamentabili Sane,* which condemned the errors of the Modernists. He followed that up with his famous encyclical *Pascendi Dominici Gregis (Against Modernism—1907)*, which condemned the evils of Modernism.[23] One of the results of this encyclical was that all priests were required to take the *Oath against Modernism*.[24] (In 1967 the Vatican replaced this Oath with a different Profession of Faith.)

After Pope St. Pius X died in 1914, Pope Benedict XV was elected and would reign until 1922. Whereas Leo XIII and St. Pius X dealt with Freemasonry and Modernism, Benedict XV had to contend with World War I and Communism, which took power in Russia in 1917 during his reign. This was also a time of great change in women's fashions.

In 1910, the Archbishop of Paris led a campaign against women's immodest fashions. Think about that for a moment! What were women wearing *in 1910* that was so bad?

Five years later the Church released a General Pastoral Directive stating that women must be dressed decently at Mass and that the priest may refuse them entrance into the church if they are not dressed properly.[25]

The fact is that in comparison to the modest fashions of just a decade or two prior to this, the new fashions displayed an alarming trend toward immodesty that was—all things considered—simply unacceptable. Viewed from our perspective, one has to wonder whether or not the Popes were privy to the plan of the fashion designers for them to have blown the whistle on the new fashions so early in the game, historically speaking.

Imagine the very conservative styles of that time period—*before* the flapper craze of the 1920's that saw short skirts to the knees and sleeveless dresses. Obviously, fashions were already changing drastically—and *not* for the better.

On May 13, 1917, Our Lady of Fatima first appeared to three children in Portugal. She would appear on the 13th of the next five months and would later tell one of the children, Blessed Jacinta Marto, that "more souls go to Hell for sins of the flesh than for any other reason."[26] This innocent young child may not have fully realized what "sins of the flesh" meant, but the Baltimore Catechism teaches us that these sins fall under the Sixth and Ninth Commandments.[27]

Our Lady of Fatima also said that certain fashions would be introduced "that will offend Our Lord very much." Jacinta commented later that people who serve God should not follow current fashion trends. Jacinta also said that the Church has no fashions, and that "Our Lord is always the same."

Also in 1917, the young St. Maximilian Kolbe was witnessing the 200th anniversary celebrations of Freemasonry in Rome. The celebrations featured banners depicting St. Michael being trodden underfoot by Satan and slogans such as "Satan will rule on Vatican

Hill, and the Pope will serve as his errand boy."[28]

St. Maximilian comments that these demonstrations simply carried out the Masonic rule of action: "Destroy all teaching about God, especially Catholic teaching."[29] The Saint continues: "The Freemasons follow this rule above all: 'Catholicism can be overcome not by logical argument but by corrupted morals.'"[30]

Corruption of morals? Where have we heard that strategy before?

That same year, St. Maximilian Kolbe founded the Knights of the Immaculata to fight the forces of Satan by spreading devotion to Mary Immaculate.

Slacks appeared on the fashion runways of Paris in 1920. The next year, Pope Benedict XV expressed his shock that women would embrace the current fashion trends and styles of dancing. He wrote,

> . . . one cannot sufficiently deplore the blindness of so many women of every age and condition; made foolish by desire to please, they do not see to what a degree the indecency of their clothing shocks every honest man, and offends God. Most of them would formerly have blushed for those toilettes [outfits] as for a grave fault against Christian modesty; now it does not suffice for them to exhibit them on the public thoroughfares; they do not fear to cross the threshold of the churches, to assist at the Holy Sacrifice of the Mass, and even to bear the seducing food of shameful passions to the Eucharistic Table where one receives the heavenly Author of purity. And We speak not of those exotic and barbarous dances recently imported into fashionable circles, one more shocking than the other; one cannot imagine anything more suitable for banishing all the remains of modesty.[31]

In the 1920's, women's clothing styles were taking on a radical and revolutionary new look. For the first time in history, women of refinement were seen wearing sleeves above the elbow and hemlines that crawled up to the knee. Remember that Masonic directive: "first, undress up to the elbow; then up to the knees; then arms and legs completely uncovered; later, the upper part of the chest, the shoulders, etc. etc." [32]

In 1928 Pope Pius XI wrote, "There is a sad forgetfulness of Christian modesty, especially in the life and dress of women." [33]

Worldly Catholics and secular society responded by saying that modesty in dress was regulated by "customs and styles of time, place and circumstances." They encouraged women to ignore these statements from the Church. Instead, they said, it was society and culture that should dictate what is modest and appropriate.

But in their publications, Freemasons had revealed their motive and plan. The following quote bears repeating:

> Religion does not fear the dagger's point; but it can vanish under corruption. Let us not grow tired of corruption: we may use a pretext, such as sport, hygiene, health resorts. It is necessary to corrupt, that our boys and girls practice nudism in dress. To avoid too much reaction, one would have to progress in a methodical manner: first, undress up to the elbow; then up to the knees; then arms and legs completely uncovered; later, the upper part of the chest, the shoulders, etc. etc. [34]

If you look at the fashion trends since 1928, you can see that styles have very closely followed this strategy. At that time, garments were already up to the elbows and knees.

The year 1928 was also the beginning of Pope Pius XI's Modesty Crusade. It makes one think that he may have known about the plan of Freemasonry.

The Modesty Crusade started with a Letter to the Bishops of Italy (August 23, 1928) and was directed primarily at schools run by religious sisters. It spoke against immodest fashions, "which prevail today to the detriment of good breeding . . ."[35]

Then on January 12, 1930, the Sacred Congregation of the Council (now called the Congregation for the Clergy), by order of Pope Pius XI, issued a Letter to the Bishops that exhorted bishops, priests, nuns, teachers, parents, etc. to insist on modesty in those under their charge. The document concludes with these words:

> Maidens and women dressed immodestly are to be debarred from Holy Communion and from acting as sponsors at the Sacraments of Baptism and Confirmation; further, if the offense be extreme, they may even be forbidden to enter the church.[36]

Detailed instructions on modesty of dress for women had been issued on September 24, 1928, by the Cardinal-Vicar (Vicar General) of Pope Pius XI in Rome, Basilio Cardinal Pompili:

> We recall that a dress cannot be called decent which is cut deeper than two fingers' breadth under the pit of the throat, which does not cover the arms at least to the elbows,* and scarcely reaches a bit beyond the knees. Furthermore, dresses of transparent material are improper.[37]

Pope Pius XII (1939-1958) continued the Modesty Crusade during his pontificate. In an allocution of May 22, 1941 to young Catholic girls during World War II, he urged them not to fall for fashions that had, until then, been worn only by "women of doubtful virtue."

---

*Short sleeves were permitted as a temporary concession, with ecclesiastical approval, because of "impossible market conditions."

His words are a sobering reminder that the Church is ever mindful of the salvation of souls.

> Numbers of believing and pious women . . . in accepting to follow certain bold fashions, break down, by their example, the resistance of many other women to such fashions, which may become for them the cause of spiritual ruin. As long as these provocative styles remain identified with women of doubtful virtue, good women do not dare to follow them; but once these styles have been accepted by women of good reputation, decent women soon follow their example, and are carried along by the tide into possible disaster.[38]

The Canadian bishops followed suit in the Spring of 1946, this time admonishing men to wear shirts in public—even at the beach—and to avoid tight trousers.[39]

That summer, 1946, the first bikini strutted its way down the runways of Paris.

Coco Chanel came back onto the fashion scene in 1954 and reintroduced her designs from the 1930's.

That summer, Pope Pius XII said,

> Now many girls do not see anything wrong with following certain shameless styles, like so many sheep. They would surely blush if they could only guess the impression they make and the feelings they arouse in those who see them.[40]

Pope Pius XII cautioned women that, if certain styles were an occasion of sin for others, it was their duty not to wear them. He also warned mothers to make sure their children were dressed modestly. His timeless admonition sounds as though it could have been written today!

The good of our soul is more important than that of our body; and we have to prefer the spiritual welfare of our neighbor to our bodily comforts . . . If a certain kind of dress constitutes a grave and proximate occasion of sin, and endangers the salvation of your soul and others, it is your duty to give it up . . .

O Christian mothers, if you knew what a future of anxieties and perils, of ill subdued doubts, of hardly suppressed shame you prepare for your sons and daughters, imprudently getting them accustomed to live scantily dressed and making them lose the sense of modesty, you would be ashamed of yourselves and you would dread the harm you are making for yourselves, the harm which you are causing these children, whom Heaven has entrusted to you to be brought up as Christians.[41]

Tragically, some mothers today are enabling their young daughters to dress in "hooker chic." Have parents become desensitized to today's fashions? Have they been duped by the fashion industry? Manipulated by wanting their children to be "popular"?

Whatever the reason, one commentator gets right to the point:

The sad fact is that a lot of today's tween and teen girls dress like streetwalkers. . . . How do so many little girls end up looking like sex objects?

How? Because their parents let them. . . .

Face the facts: Most 12 to 16-year-olds don't have access to a lot of cash—unless, of course, their parents give it to them. . . . And it's usually the mom who happily drives the little darlings to the mall for a fun day of shopping. Face it: Little girls dress according to what their mommies allow.

I thought mothers were supposed to protect their daughters, to teach them to value themselves and their bodies. What chance does a little girl stand of keeping her childhood or innocence intact when it's mommy that's driving her to the store and paying for the thongs, the itty-bitty skirts, the hipster jeans and the plunging necklines?

And when did fathers start letting their precious little girls dress like "ladies of the night"? Hello, is anybody out there?[42]

Do parents realize that "ladies of the night" wouldn't wear on street corners in the 1950's what some girls wear to the mall these days?

So let's get back to the 1950's.

Pope Pius XII recognized that women are the moral fiber of society, and he knew that the culture would implode if modesty were not put into practice. "Society reveals what it is by the clothes it wears," Pius XII said in 1954. ". . . An unworthy, indecent mode of dress has prevailed" without any distinction of place, "on beaches, in country resorts, on the streets, etc. Vice necessarily follows upon public nudity . . ."[43]

The Pope wasn't the only one who had something to say about fashion's downward spiral. Everyday clothing was using less and less material, and going to the beach was a relatively new pastime that was gaining in popularity. In 1959, Cardinal Pla y Daniel, Archbishop of Toledo, Spain, stated,

> A special danger to morals is represented by public bathing at beaches . . . Mixed bathing between men and women, which is nearly always a proximate occasion of sin and a scandal, must be avoided.[44]

The Cardinal was simply echoing and reinforcing what the Roman Emperors knew two thousand years ago: mixed swimming leads to promiscuity. That's a long way from where our culture is today, isn't it!

Cardinal Siri, of Genoa, Italy, wrote a letter in 1960

called "Notification Concerning Men's Dress Worn by Women." He expressed concern that by wearing trousers, women were imitating and competing with men. His concern was that this would bring about in women the mental attitudes of a man, and would modify a woman's gestures, attitudes and behavior. (The Cardinal's entire letter is included here as Appendix Three.)

Every woman I know acknowledges that when she's wearing a dress, she moves and acts differently from when she is wearing pants.

A story about St. Padre Pio and women's fashions is told by Anne McGinn Cillis, a Canadian and a spiritual daughter of the Saint. In her book, *Arrivederci, Padre Pio: "A Spiritual Daughter Remembers,"* Mrs. Cillis relates:

> I had occasion in April of 1963 to interview, in San Giovanni Rotondo, a Canadian lady, Italian by descent and fluent in the language of her forebearers, who had been refused absolution in Confession by Padre Pio because she sold slacks and pant-suits in her dress shop in Vancouver.
>
> He commanded her to return home to Canada and dispose of *all* this stock, and not to give any of the items to people who might wear them, and if she wanted his absolution, she could come back to Italy and receive it, *only* after she had ruthlessly carried out his orders.
>
> The alternative was, she could seek the absolution in another Confession, back in Canada, but he, Padre Pio, would *know* whether she had done what she'd been told.[45] [Emphasis in original.]

How did the dress shop owner take this? She was "thunderstruck" by Padre Pio's words, but then decided to do as he had directed. In fact, she expressed a vigorous determination to carry out Padre Pio's instruc-

tions.[46] In her book, Mrs. Cillis notes that Padre Pio
was also firm about modesty for men and boys, but
that he was "especially adamant on the wearing of
slacks (and shorts) by women."[47]

St. Padre Pio refused women access to the confessional if their dresses were too short. On the door of
the church was this message:

> By Padre Pio's explicit wish, women must enter
> the confessional wearing skirts at least 8 inches below
> the knee. It is forbidden to borrow longer dresses in
> church and to wear them for the Confessional.[48]

As one author commented, while fashion designers
had skirts climbing to more than eight inches above
the knee, Padre Pio warned women to keep their skirts
eight inches *below* the knee.

What have we heard more recently from the Vatican about modesty or fashions?

The Vatican's 1975 *Declaration on Certain Questions
concerning Sexual Ethics*, in addressing the problem
of solitary sin against purity, stated that this was linked
with various causes, including "the neglect of modesty,
which is the guardian of chastity." The document urged
"the observance of modesty" as one of the means to
live a chaste life.[49]

The Pontifical Council for the Family stated the following to parents in 1995 regarding dressing with dignity and modesty:

> Also of importance are what Christian tradition has
> called the younger sisters of chastity (modesty, an
> attitude of sacrifice with regard to one's whims),
> nourished by the faith and a life of prayer.
>   *The practice of decency and modesty* in speech,
> action and dress is very important for creating an
> atmosphere suitable to the growth of chastity, but
> this must be well motivated by respect for one's own

body and the dignity of others. Parents, as we have said, should be watchful so that certain immoral fashions and attitudes do not violate the integrity of the home, especially through misuse of the *mass media*. . . . Respect for *privacy* must be considered in close connection with decency and modesty, which spontaneously defend a person who refuses to be considered and treated like an object of pleasure instead of being respected and loved for himself or herself. . . . Even if they are socially acceptable, some habits of speech and dress are not morally correct and represent a way of trivializing sexuality, reducing it to a consumer object. Parents should therefore teach their children the value of Christian modesty, moderate dress, and when it comes to trends, the necessary autonomy.[50]

More recently, *The Catechism of the Catholic Church* had a number of things to say about modesty in dress and behavior. These passages are the most pertinent:

Purity requires *modesty*, an integral part of temperance. Modesty protects the intimate center of the person. It means refusing to unveil what should remain hidden. It is ordered to chastity, to whose sensitivity it bears witness. It guides how one looks at others and behaves toward them in conformity with the dignity of persons and their solidarity. (2521). Modesty protects the mystery of persons and their love. . . . Modesty is decency. It inspires one's choice of clothing. (2522). Modesty inspires a way of life which makes it possible to resist the allurements of fashion and prevailing ideologies. (2523). The forms taken by modesty vary from one culture to another. Everywhere, however, modesty exists as an intuition of the spiritual dignity proper to man. It is born with the awakening consciousness of being a subject. Teaching modesty to children and adolescents means awakening in them respect for the human person. (2524).[51]

We can see that over the years, Holy Mother Church has seen fit to educate and warn the faithful about fashion trends and about the gravity of immodest and undignified behavior and dress.

We have the evidence that today's fashions are the result of planning by those whose goal is the total destruction of Christian society. But we have also been advised as to what path to take. It's up to us to use our free will and decide what to do for our families and ourselves.

As women's fashions have fallen into the gutters, many women have lost the knowledge of what it means to be feminine. *It certainly doesn't mean being prissy.* So, what is femininity?

NOTES

1. Freemasonry is a secret society which was founded in England in 1717. Freemasons have secret doctrines, rituals and oaths. They consider Masonry to be the *universal* religion, and they honor Jesus Christ as they honor Socrates, Buddha and Mohammed. Freemasonry claims that Christ is not divine and that Satan is not evil. (Bro. Charles Madden, O.F.M. Conv., *Freemasonry: Mankind's Hidden Enemy.* Rockford, IL: TAN, 1995, especially pp. 46, 48, 8).
2. Hermann Gruber, "Masonry," *The Catholic Encyclopedia*, Vol. IX, Robert Appleton Company, 1910, p. 786.
3. Speech of Msgr. Jouin, Dec. 8, 1930. www.catholicism.org/pages/jouin/htm
4. Gruber, *op. cit.*, p. 787.
5. Jouin, *op. cit.*
6. *Ibid.*
7. Pope Leo XIII, *Humanum Genus,* par. 20, 1884, TAN reprint 1978, p. 12.
8. Canon Law Society of America, *Code of Canon Law* (Washington, DC: CLSA, 1983), p. 497. An "interdict" is a Catholic Church penalty whereby Catholics, while remaining members of the Church, are excluded from certain sacred offices and from reception or administration of specified Sacraments of the Church. (Cf. Attwater, *A Catholic Dictionary,* p. 259.)

9. "Declaration on Masonic Associations" by the Sacred Congregation for the Doctrine of the Faith, Nov. 26, 1983, quoted in Madden, *op. cit.,* Appendix B, p. 31.

10. In 1818, a member of the Illuminati, Nubius, stated that their goal was "the destruction forever of Catholicism and even of the Christian idea, which, if left standing on the ruins of Rome, would be the resuscitation of Christianity later on." Quoted by Msgr. Dillon (see note 14 below), p. 52.

11. www.catholicism.org/pages/phantom.htm

12. John Vennari, *The Permanent Instruction of the Alta Vendita,* TAN, 1999, p. 10.

13. "The task that we are going to undertake is not the work of a day, or of a month, or of a year; it may last several years, perhaps a century; but in our ranks the soldier dies and struggle goes on . . ." Vennari, *op. cit.,* pp. 6-7.

14. Letter of Vindex to Nubius (pen names of two leaders of the *Alta Vendita,* the highest lodge of the Italian Carbonari, Masonic revolutionaries), Aug. 9, 1838. Quoted in Monsignor George F. Dillon, D.D., *Grand Orient Freemasonry Unmasked* (Dublin: Gill, 1885; reprint, Palmdale, CA: Christian Book Club, 1999), p. 64. (This book bears two Imprimaturs: one from 1885 and one from 1950.)

15. Pearl Buck, cited in Alice von Hildebrand, *op. cit.,* p. 28.

16. "The Illuminati had . . . a plan . . . they decided on a most ambitious line of conduct. It would form and control public opinion. It would amalgamate religions by dissolving all the differences of belief and ritual that had kept them apart; and it would take over the Papacy and place an agent of its own in the Chair of Peter." Piers Compton, *The Broken Cross,* 1981, pp. 7-8. Quoted by www.cuttingedge.org

17. Canon Francis Ripley, *This Is The Faith,* Third Edition (1951; Rockford, IL: TAN, 2002), pp. 91-92. This book gives a good explanation of the classic Catholic principles regarding sins against purity and modesty. Other good explanations are found in *A Brief Catechism for Adults,* by Fr. William J. Cogan (TAN, 1993) and in *Hell—Plus How to Avoid Hell,* by Fr. Schouppe and Thomas A. Nelson (TAN, 1989).

18. Interestingly, it was almost exactly 100 years later—Oct. 3, 1984—that Pope John Paul II issued the document *Quattor Abhinc Annos,* commonly called "the Indult," by which the Traditional Latin Mass slowly began to be re-introduced into the Church at large, after having been, in effect, banned since 1969.

19. Story based on various sources, including the websites http://members.aol.com/bjw1106/marian7a.html http://www.stjosephschurch.net/leoxiii.html, and conversations with various priests and other Catholics.

20. The Prayer to St. Michael the Archangel was said after each

Low Mass from that day forward until the introduction of the *Novus Ordo* Mass in 1969. The prayer is as follows: "Saint Michael the Archangel, defend us in battle; be our defense against the wickedness and snares of the devil. May God rebuke him, we humbly pray; and do thou, O Prince of the heavenly host, by the power of God, thrust into Hell Satan and the other evil spirits, who prowl about the world seeking the ruin of souls. Amen."

21. It is said that Cardinal Rampolla was listed on the *Ordo Templi Orientis'* Manifesto—its list of members, or at least supporters. (Craig Heimbichner, "Did a Freemason Almost Become Pope? The story of Cardinal Rampolla," in *Catholic Family News*, Aug., 2003). www.cfnews.org

22. "Suddenly the conclave was interrupted by a shock: Jan Cardinal Puzyna, Bishop of Cracow (at that time within the Austrian Empire), rose to give a declaration which stunned the assembly. In Latin he declared '. . . officially and in the name and by the authority of Franz-Josef, Emperor of Austria and King of Hungary, that His Majesty, in virtue of an ancient right and privilege, pronounces the veto of exclusion against my Most Eminent Lord, Cardinal Mariano Rampolla del Tindaro.'" Heimbichner, *op. cit.,* quoting Yves Chiron, *Saint Pius X: Restorer of the Church* (Kansas City, MO: Angelus Press, 2002), p. 122.

23. Pope St. Pius X said that Modernism was "the synthesis all heresies." (*Pascendi*, par. 39). The *Catholic Encyclopedia* boils Modernism down to "the critique of our supernatural knowledge according to the false postulates of contemporary philosophy." Toward the end of his encyclical, St. Pius X declares, "Make no mistake about it, Venerable Brethren, they [the Modernists] plan to change everything."

24. "The Oath against Modernism," "*Pascendi*," "*Lamentabili*" and "*The Syllabus of Errors*" of Pope Pius IX are included in *The Popes Against Modern Errors: 16 Papal Documents*, Edited by Anthony J. Mioni, Jr., TAN, 1999.

25. The General Pastoral Directive of 1915 states, "Women must be decently dressed, especially when they go to church. The parish priest may, with due prudence, refuse them entrance to the church and access to the reception of the Sacraments, any and every time that they come to church immodestly dressed."

26. Cf. Msgr. Joseph A. Cirrincione, *Ven. Jacinta Marto of Fatima* (Rockford, IL: TAN, 1992), p. 54. Cf. this work also for the words of Jacinta in the following paragraph.

27. The Sixth Commandment is "Thou shalt not commit adultery." The Ninth Commandment is "Thou shalt not covet thy neighbor's wife."

    " 'Lust' is the desire for sins of the flesh; for impure thoughts, words, or actions. It comes under the Sixth and Ninth Commandments, and includes all that is forbidden by those Commandments. It is the habit of always violating, or of desiring to violate, the Sixth and Ninth Commandments. Lust and impurity mean the same thing. The *followers of lust* are, generally, neglect of prayer, neglect of the Sacraments, and final loss of faith." (*An Explanation of the Baltimore Catechism of Christian Doctrine* (also known as *Baltimore Catechism No. 4*), by Rev. Thomas L. Kinkead, 1891; TAN Books and Publishers, Inc., Rockford, IL, 1988, p. 62).

28. St. Maximilian Kolbe, Appendix A (with translator's note of Fr. Bernard Geiger, O.F.M. Conv.) of *Freemasonry: Mankind's Hidden Enemy*, by Bro. Charles Madden, O.F.M. Conv. (Rockford, IL: TAN, 1995), pp. 29-30.

29. *Ibid.*

30. *Ibid.*
    These words of St. Maximilian Kolbe have become famous: "Modern times are dominated by Satan and will be more so in the future. The conflict with Hell cannot be engaged by men, even the most clever. The Immaculata alone has from God the promise of victory over Satan." (*St. Maximilian Kolbe: Knight of the Immaculata*, by Fr. Jeremiah J. Smith, O.F.M. Conv., 1952; TAN, 1998, p. 16).

31. Encyclical *Sacra Propediem*, Jan. 6, 1921, par. 19.
    www.vatican.va/holy_father/benedict_xv/encyclicals/document

32. *International Review on Freemasonry*, 1928.

33. Pope Pius XI, Encyclical Letter *Miserentissimus Redemptor*— "Reparation to the Sacred Heart," no. 16.

34. *International Review on Freemasonry*, 1928.

35. Article "Rome's Decrees on Modesty . . ." (See note 36).

36. *Acta Apostolica Sedis*, 1930, Vol. 22, pp. 26-28; also, *Canon Law Digest*, 1, pp. 212-214. Cited in article "Rome's Decrees on Modesty in Dress Are Still Victims of 'Conspiracy of Silence,'" a reprint from *The Marylike Crusader*, Nov.-Dec. 1963, a publication of The Marylike Crusade, Bartelso, IL (also Rathdrum, ID).

37. "Rome's Decrees . . .," *op. cit.* According to Father Kunkel, this document (the "Roman Standard" of modesty) was originally published in the *Bulletin of the Roman Clergy*, Oct., 1928. Father Bernard A. Kunkel, *Marylike Modesty Handbook of the Purity Crusade of Mary Immaculate*, orig. edition circa 1955, new edition published as part of *My Life in Prayer Book* (Pittsburgh: Radio Rosary, 1998), p. 247.

38. Pope Pius XII, Allocution to the Girls of Catholic Action, May 22, 1941, par. 67. (This passage is found, in a different translation, in *WMW*, p. 60.)

39. "Man himself does not escape from the inclination of exhibiting his flesh: some go in public, stripped to the waist, or in

very tight pants or in very scanty bathing suits. They thus commit offenses against the virtue of modesty. They may also be an occasion of sin (in thought or desire) for our neighbor." May, 1946.

40. Allocution to Children of Mary Immaculate, July 17, 1954, par. 443, in *WMW*, p. 228 (different translation).

41. Pius XII, Allocution to the Girls of Catholic Action, May 22, 1941, par. 67. (This passage is found, in a different translation, in *WMW*, p. 60.)

42. Rebecca Hagelin, "America's little girls . . . or tramps?" World Net Daily, Mar. 4, 2005. www.wnd.com/news/article. Excerpts from this article appeared in *The Washington Times*, March 21-27, 2005, p. 28.

43. August 29, 1954, quoted in *The Fatima Crusader*, No. 57, p. 53.

44. Quoted in Kunkel, *op. cit.*, pp. 248-249.

45. Anne McGinn Cillis, *Arrivederci, Padre Pio: "A Spiritual Daughter Remembers"—A Book of Lifetime Memories* (Ottawa: The Archangel Press, 2003), p. 1432.

46. Telephone interview of Anne Cillis by TAN staff.

47. Cillis, *Arrivederci*, p. 1432.

48. "Padre Pio wouldn't tolerate low-necked dresses or short, tight skirts, and he forbade his spiritual daughters to wear transparent stockings. Each year his severity increased. He stubbornly dismissed them from his confessional, even before they set foot inside, if he judged them to be improperly dressed. On some mornings he drove away one after another, until he ended up hearing very few confessions.

    "His brothers observed these drastic purges with a certain uneasiness and decided to fasten a sign on the church door: 'By Padre Pio's explicit wish, women must enter his confessional wearing skirts at least eight inches below the knees. It is forbidden to borrow longer dresses in church and to wear them for the confessional.'" Dorothy Gaudiose, *Prophet of the People: A Biography of Padre Pio* (Staten Island, NY: Alba House, 1974), pp. 191-192.

49. Sacred Congregation for the Doctrine of the Faith, "Declaration on Certain Questions concerning Sexual Ethics," Dec. 29, 1975, Sections IX, XII. http://www.vatican.va

50. "Truth and Meaning of Human Sexuality," Dec. 8, 1995, Pontifical Council for the Family, nos. 55, 56, 57, 97. http://www.vatican.va (Emphasis in original).

51. *Catechism of the Catholic Church*, 2nd Ed. (Washington, DC: U.S. Catholic Conference, 1997), p. 604. (Emphasis in original.)

CHAPTER FIVE

Return to Femininity

BEING feminine does not mean being giggly, unintelligent, incompetent or unreliable. It doesn't mean that you are required to wear clothing that has ribbons, bows, ruffles or lace.

Instead, our femininity is an assignment from God. It is how God created us. It is a character that is imprinted deeply upon us, which is made apparent in our physical bodies, and by how we speak, act and dress.

We were not created *men*. We were created to be *women*! And we must be *strong* women—in accord with God's Will for us. How?

As the translator of Cardinal Siri's warning to his clergy comments, "When a woman is feminine, she has the strength God gives her. But when she is de-feminized, she has only the strength she gives herself."[1]

By trying to blur the divinely created differences between men and women, our culture has succeeded in destroying the integrity of both.

The Church teaches that *men and women are equal in dignity, yet separate in role and function*, and that those roles and functions are *complementary*!

It is similar to our having two eyes. The left eye sees the world from one angle. The right eye sees the same world, but just a bit differently. Yet when we use both eyes, we are able to see a beautiful, three-dimensional picture of the world![2]

It's the same in marriage. The husband and wife

have their own view of the world and make their own unique contribution to the marriage. At the same time, they co-operate with each other and should not try to take over the other's role.[3]

"Mankind cannot accomplish its mission in a merely masculine way, nor can it accomplish it in a merely feminine way."[4] It's the balance of masculinity and femininity that helps us attain our common goals. And it's not just in marriage that this male-female balance exists. St. Francis of Assisi and St. Claire supported each other in the foundation of the Franciscan Order, as did St. Francis de Sales and St. Jane Frances de Chantal in the foundation of the Visitation Order and the twins St. Benedict and St. Scholastica in the foundation of the Benedictine Order.

Women help men by developing their emotions and manners, so that men can balance out their analytical nature. Chesterton says it's the feminine dignity against masculine rowdiness, and that if women do not insist on good manners, everyone knows that nobody else will![5]

Men, however, bring stability to a woman's world. Since they don't take their feelings quite so seriously as we take ours,[6] men can help us women look at things in a more practical way.

We should bring to life our womanliness, which in turn will let our men magnify their masculinity. After all, in the normal scheme of things, a man is attracted to a woman, not to another guy. Opposites attract! And principled men are quick to encourage women to be proud of that which God created them to be—namely, *women!*

Ladies, it's time for us to be counter-cultural—*counter to our misguided contemporary culture, that is!*

It's a fact that virtuous and moral women who display compassion attract thoughtful men who have character, patience and generosity. In marriage, as a woman grows in virtue and in her Faith, "the unbelieving husband is sanctified by the believing wife," as St. Paul says. (*1 Corinthians* 7:14).

By the same token, badly behaving women will often attract selfish, shallow and immoral men.

What sort of men do we want as husbands for our daughters? Thoughtful men with character, patience and generosity . . . or amoral slobs who are only out for themselves?

Young men do not develop their social skills as easily or as early as young women. When they are in their teens, young men tend to be more comfortable around girls who are a bit tomboyish.

But as these same young men mature and are interested in courting, they are attracted to their exact opposite. Young men with character admire femininity, purity, charm and a joyful attitude in the women who attract them. All of this awakens their chivalrous nature, and they develop a warm and loving desire to protect and shelter their "maiden" from harm—to admire her and cherish her, to be "her knight in shining armor."

When was the last time you asked for help and a man turned his back on your need? When a woman gently asks a man for help, he rises to the occasion like a medieval knight. It's called "chivalry," and believe it or not, *it still exists*!

But we women don't realize what our real feminine charms are. We might look at another woman who is fashionably (even immodestly) dressed, in perfect shape, witty and bold and think that most men would like that.

Instead, men with character are attracted to the virtuous qualities in a woman. They admire her joy, her inner happiness, her femininity, her playful spunk.

Men will read our body language and will respond to what they perceive. If we carry ourselves with the

style and grace of Princess Diana, men pick up on that.
If we carry ourselves like a floozy, men pick up on that
as well.

Femininity, style and grace are more than just what
we wear on the outside. They are also about who we
are and what God has created us to be on the inside
as well.

When we think of "modesty" we usually think of the
way someone dresses, or the way someone behaves.
"She dresses very modestly, doesn't she?" Or, "He's a
great athlete, and yet he's so modest!"

But that is only a *part* of what modesty is all about!
Modesty is a portion of the virtue of Temperance—"the
restraining virtue, the virtue that regulates our impul-
sive urges and holds us back from going too far"[7] with
any kind of passion or activity. Temperance makes sure
that our desires and acts observe the mode of reason
and do not exceed their proper bounds.[8] The root word
of "modesty" is "mode," as in moderation. That means
we avoid the extremes—not too much and not too little. As the saying goes, *Virtus in medio stat*—"Virtue
stands in the middle." The word "virtue" comes from
the Latin *virtus*, meaning strength and manliness.

Included in the virtue of Temperance we find humility, reverence for God, studiousness, restraint of our
passions, being in control of our emotions, purity,
chastity and modesty in dress (not only for women,
but for men, too!).

A comment I hear from some women is that they
feel they ought to be able to wear whatever they want,
and it's the man's fault if he is offended or if he looks.
Would you consider that attitude a lack of humility?
Wouldn't that be the same as saying, "What I want is
more important than what you may need"?

Instead, shouldn't we, in charity and humility, be
concerned about the welfare of others? St. Paul said
in his letter to the Romans, "But judge this rather,

that you put not a stumbling block or a scandal in your brother's way." (*Romans* 14:13).

John Kamprath, the Director of Professional Development for the National Association of Private Catholic and Independent Schools, has done a magnificent "Virtue's Workshop," which he has graciously shared with me for this book.[9]

Mr. Kamprath compares the virtues to a ladder reaching to Heaven. The rungs are all the little things we do to form good habits. As we climb the ladder, we find resting places (or platforms) that are the virtues themselves. He says that in order to form children properly, the base of that ladder needs to be Temperance—specifically humility, studiousness and modest speech, dress and bodily movements. Then you move on to Fortitude, Justice, Prudence, Faith, Hope and Charity.

That brings us to what we typically think about when we think of "modesty"—how we speak, how we dress and how we move our bodies.

St. Thomas Aquinas teaches that the outward movements of the body pertain to the beauty of moral goodness.[10] He says that bodily movements are actually virtuous when they are fitting for the person performing them and for the other persons, places and occupations involved.

Our speech too should be directed by Temperance. And to be friendly and joyful in speech is a form of kindness toward others. Our speech may change, depending on where we are. Decorum will dictate if we say anything, and how we say it. St. Benedict identifies twelve degrees of humility, which include speaking few words and maintaining silence until asked for an opinion.

Now, for how we dress. Outward things—such as clothing and adornments—are not in and of themselves either virtuous or vicious. It's how they are used! (An obvious exception would be inherently evil objects.)

In his "Virtues Workshop," Mr. Kamprath gives one of the best explanations of moderation in dress that I have ever heard. He says that men and women shouldn't be overly attached to or pleased with what they wear. Clothing shouldn't be so flashy or bold that it attracts attention to ourselves, and we should be satisfied and content with what we have, for example, not buying a new coat each year when our old one is just fine. Basically, we should keep it simple.

But in keeping it simple, we must also be cautious not to go too far the other way! Remember, it's about moderation. Not too much one way, not too much the other.

Take, for example, someone who purposely "dresses down." This person ignores everyday decorum and dresses in a sloppy, careless manner. Maybe this is done on purpose in an attempt to show disregard for vanity, but what people like this end up doing is drawing undue attention to themselves, which is a lack of humility. "Dressing down" or looking frumpy is *not* a sign of holiness! Remember—everything in moderation!

And there are those who say that modesty is simply determined by what the culture says it is. I don't know about you, but *I refuse to take modesty advice from our present culture of death!* We currently do not live in a sane world, so we cannot use our present culture as a guidepost. We must instead turn to the wisdom of the ages, which gives us the particulars of clothing and adornment that is dignified and modest. We'll get into those particulars in the next chapter.

We know that true beauty comes from within and shines out through our eyes, which are the windows of our souls. The Ancient Greeks, too, understood inner beauty to be virtue. *Let me repeat*, femininity, style and grace are more than just what we wear on the outside. They are also about who we are and what God created us to be on the inside as well. So let's look at inner femininity.

Women by nature are especially gifted to be receptive.[11] According to Webster's dictionary, receptivity means to be open and responsive to ideas, impressions or suggestions. That could mean showing an interest in something beautiful, or showing an interest in and concern for others.

Both men and women are receptive to some extent because they share the same human nature, and everyone, both men and women, possesses, to some degree, all the characteristics of being human. But women are more comfortable and at home in the role of being receptive than men generally are, and "move in it with ease and grace."[12]

Part of our feminine receptivity is to be concerned with people, the practical, the immediate, the here and now. A man's tendency is to be concerned with concepts, how things work, and the big picture.

For example, women's interests are centered on the human side of our lives: our family, relationships, concerns about health, welfare and the spiritual well-being of our children's souls.[13] These are all human concerns, and when we get together with other women, this is what we talk about.

When men get together, they speak about ideas and things such as politics, the economy, cars and sports.

As Chesterton said, "Women speak to each other; men speak to the subject they are speaking about."[14]

Men solve problems, provide and protect.

Women are intuitive and don't need (or take!) much time to think before they respond. We put real people above abstract thoughts. We help. We vent. We care. We worry. We cry. Boy, do we cry!

Because of our receptivity, we are more likely to be emotionally wounded than men. Men's analytical nature helps protect them from negative feelings.[15]

But our tears can be holy. Tears shed out of self-ishness are not holy. Some tears are silly, selfish and illegitimate, and yet we can't seem to stop them![16]

But when we cry when God is offended, children are starving, or people are unjustly killed, that is a proper response to sin in the world. Christ wept when His friend Lazarus died. He also said, "Blessed are they who mourn." (*Matthew* 5:5). We should all pray for holy tears—tears shed out of love, gratitude and contrition.[17]

When you come right down to it, women's God-given femininity includes the fact that we are communicative, nurturing, sensitive, generous, caring, loving and supportive. It's what makes us the heart of the home!

"A woman's way to holiness is clearly to purify her God-given sensitivity and to direct it into the proper channels."[18] When we're living in accordance with Natural Law—which is the Law that God has built into His creation, and that operates even though a person doesn't understand it or believe in it—we're happy. It's only when we violate Natural Law that it brings us unhappiness, ugliness and destruction.

It's interesting to note that the Feminist Movement has violated the Natural Law in a big way: Instead of promoting true femininity over mannishness, it has unintentionally conceded the superiority of men by denying women their femininity and trying to make us wish we were all men.[19] The "feminists" encourage us to act like men in our clothing choices, mannerisms and language—in other words, to be something we are not and were never created to be. What we have to ask ourselves, Ladies, is this: *"What's wrong with being feminine?"*

When we hear the word "femininity," we normally think about how a woman speaks, moves and dresses—in other words, her outer appearance.

But a woman who is comfortable with her femininity also has an inner attitude of femininity. She doesn't mind being dependent on a man for some things. After all, it is natural that at some times in a woman's life she must depend on her husband to take care of things, especially during those times after the birth of a new child.

Genuine, God-given, inner femininity appeals to men. It stirs up in them their genuine, innate masculinity and the desire to protect, revere and defend the gentle sex.

Women tend to care a bit too much about clothing, fashions, and their hair and make-up (as men tend to care too much about competition and sports). But paying attention to grooming is not wrong, so long as we don't go overboard. St. Thomas Aquinas says that your clothing should be consistent with your state in life.[20]

Besides, all fashions have a focal point. Your garments ought not to make your body the focal point, but should attract attention to your face.

Think about how our Blessed Mother is always dressed in her famous apparitions—in long, flowing, beautiful gowns that have a sash around her waist. Many times, her dresses are embroidered and decorated . . . but they are never gaudy. She is never dressed in frumpy, dowdy or shabby clothing. I'm not saying that we ought to dress like a Marian apparition, but we should use Mary as an example and wear beautiful, attractive and gracious clothing.

With our outer appearance, we want to accentuate our differences from men as much as possible. Men are linear. Women are curvy.

The book *Fascinating Womanhood* by Helen Andelin has many good recommendations about dressing and moving in a feminine manner. Interestingly enough, she recounts many of the same things we taught the students in the model school where I worked. Here are some highlights:

Pick long, flowing styles that accentuate (but don't cling to) the curves of your feminine form. Be careful not to get anything that fits tightly. (See Chapter 6 for Outfit Guidelines.) Not only are tight clothes undignified, they're just plain uncomfortable! There's nothing more awkward or more uncomfortable than having to walk around in clothing that you are constantly pulling and tugging at.

Choose feminine clothing, and stay away from anything masculine—or even unisex! Men don't wear delicate, flowing styles. Women are free to. Look for softly styled blouses, skirts that ripple when you walk, dresses that drape nicely.

If you don't own any dresses, start with an attractive one for Mass. Build from there.

Have you ever noticed how differently we move and act when we're wearing a swooshy dress? We glide around and have an air of royalty about us. For those women who have worn nothing but pants all their lives, this will be a new experience. For example, you'll need to be mindful of things that may never have crossed your mind before—like keeping your knees together when you're sitting. The longer the dress or skirt, the more comfortable you will feel that you're not showing "too much" when you're sitting down.

When you think about feminine fabrics, silk probably comes to mind. But other fabrics, such as a delicate cotton or wool, are lovely as well. What about lace, satin, chiffon, angora, and organdie?[21] Some women may not feel comfortable in these types of fabrics, but try some on anyway to see if they work for you!

A great start is a nightgown that is silky, lacy and feminine. If your husband isn't used to your wearing nightgowns, give him time, and I'll bet you that he'll love it. Dump the T-shirts, boxers and masculine-looking pajamas. And what about wearing a nightgown during winter? Just slip on some long underwear under the nightgown. You'll be amazed at how warm and cozy you'll feel!

When looking at colors in your clothing, avoid drab shades that men would use. Instead, pick materials with feminine colors and patterns. Just be careful the materials are not gaudy, loud or tasteless.

Sometimes you can soften with accessories what may be masculine-looking. Scarves, flower pins and feminine jewelry can gussy up an outfit inexpensively.

What about make-up? Whether you wear make-up or not is a personal choice. If you do, don't overdo it. Make-up should enhance your God-given features, not overshadow them. Use a light touch when applying cosmetics. St. Thomas Aquinas says that make-up is okay if you're hiding a disfigurement arising from some cause such as sickness or the like.[22] But keep it natural-looking and not fake or phony.

Women have always used some forms of cosmetics and perfume. But these days, the fashion and make-up industries have gone to the extreme; however, neglecting your appearance is not dignified either. Proper skin care is extremely important. And, not to overlook the obvious, make sure your hair is clean and arranged, and your clothing neat in appearance.

One last note: Get an apron to wear in the kitchen. Don't laugh! It's amazing how different you will feel in an apron. And, for some reason, most men love it!

How about feminine mannerisms? Picture a woman who is dressed in a Scarlet O'Hara type of gown, with her hair artfully coiffed. She is poised at the top of a long set of stairs, gazing around the room below her. She gives off an air of grace and style.

Suddenly she shouts down the stairs, "Hi, Mary!" She waves her arms brusquely in the air, then comes galloping down the steps like a horse on a mission.

Certainly you wouldn't expect that sort of behavior

from such an elegantly dressed lady. Those actions don't fit the outfit, do they? Her mannerisms would not be in harmony with her feminine clothing, and she would look amusing, shoddy and ridiculous.

Regardless of how we dress, we always want to walk, talk and use our hands, voice and facial expressions, and laugh[23] in a manner that corresponds to our inner femininity. Be proud of the woman you are, and act accordingly.

When we walk, we want to move smoothly through the air in a straight line, without much body movement, and with no hip movement! Did you ever walk with a book on your head when you were a little girl? Even if you haven't, get out that hardbound dictionary and give it a try.

Have you ever seen a woman walking slightly bent forward with her knees bent—almost like she's pushing an invisible stroller? Make sure you stand up straight and tall (there's your mother's advice again!). When walking, keep your legs almost straight and swing them directly from your hips and out in front of you. Straight legs are far more graceful. Also, remember to take smaller steps (especially if you're wearing high heels!) Make sure you don't swing your hips from side to side. If you're not too shy, ask a friend to watch you as you walk. Or, if you want, have her video you walking—from the front and from behind. Is your stride graceful and feminine, or is it more like an athlete on his way to a competition?

How about going up and down steps? Your head should not bob up and down, but glide smoothly. You'll need to bend your knees a bit more (and keep them bent) in order to achieve this.

When picking up something off the floor, don't bend from the waist and leave your bottom sticking up in the air. Instead, bend your knees and crouch down to get close to the floor.

Practice moving your hands in a flowing and graceful manner like a ballerina.

Hand shakes should be gentle, but firm. And when shaking hands with a man, don't try to out-squeeze him—unless your goal is to break his hand, or just impress him with your grip—because you are probably well out of your league . . . and besides, it is just not expected, nor feminine.

Modulate your voice to harmonize with your genteel mannerisms. Just as many women may be uncomfortable with a man with an effeminate-sounding tone of voice, most men do not like a loud, brassy-sounding woman, either.[24] Speak clearly and gently, but with confidence. Feel free to laugh!

Ah, laughter. This was tough for me, because I don't have the "tinkling laugh" you read about in books. The important point is not to be coarse or too loud.

Men also don't like being around chatty, nervous women who are always talking and twitching and bouncing around. Instead, create an aura of mystique with an economy of movement. How? Well, think of how gracefully a cat wakes up, stretches, blinks, and then gently walks away. Cats have an aura of regalness about them, don't they?

No honorable man likes a nasty-tempered woman, and on the other hand, he will probably also find it hard to respect a woman who lets others walk all over her.

One last point: femininity doesn't depend on beauty of face or figure. As Helen Andelin says, "The presence or the absence of beauty is of minor consequence in the attainment of true femininity." And in fact, even a woman who may not consider herself pretty can be "highly fascinating" to the opposite sex.[25] So, work with what you've got!

Be the feminine woman that God created you to be, and you'll find that men around you will live up to their masculine role as well. But ultimately, the choice about how you dress and carry yourself as a woman is up to you.

So where do you think our culture got the idea that dressing scantily empowers women? We know it wasn't from Our Lord. So if it doesn't come from Christ, then it must be coming from His enemy . . . and ours!

It sure seems obvious to me that Satan has used fashion designers and the clothing industry to cause many men and women to sin against the Sixth and Ninth Commandments, just as Our Lady warned Bl. Jacinta at Fatima. And I'm angry at myself that I fell for those lies and used to dress in a less than modest manner—potentially tempting men to sin.

The good news is that now I'm empowered with the truth and have made the decision to make different clothing choices for myself and my children. Do I want to passively follow the culture of death? Or do I want to help rebuild a Christian culture—one outfit at a time?

In an address to a congress of the Latin Union of High Fashion (November 8, 1957), Pope Pius XII commented on this very point:

> It is often said, almost with passive resignation, that fashions reflect the customs of a people. But it would be more exact and much more useful to say that they express the decision and moral direction that a nation intends to take: either to be shipwrecked in licentiousness or to maintain itself at the level to which it has been raised by religion and civilization.[26]

Back in 1919, Pope Benedict XV expressed his hope that Catholic women would use their influence to save *all of society*:

It was said that the faithfulness of a woman brought back to the path of justice the husband who had gone astray: 'the unbelieving husband is sanctified by the believing wife.' (*1 Corinthians* 7:14). May it soon be possible to repeat of the whole of society that it returned to the path of salvation through the example, the teaching, the mission of the Catholic woman.[27]

We women have the power to take our society in the direction in which *we want it to go*. It won't be easy at first, but with God's grace we are strong—and with Our Lord, through His Blessed Mother, we can do it! The hand that rocks the cradle really *does* rule the world!

Now it's time to take a look in your closet and break some old habits and start some new ones. But how can you tell if an outfit in your closet is going to accentuate your feminine dignity? It's not as hard as you may think!

NOTES

1. Translator's Note 7, Appendix Three, p. 136.
2. Ed Willock, "Men, Mary and Manliness," in *Fatherhood and Family: Reclaiming the Catholic Head of the Family for Our Lord Jesus Christ*, Volume 3 from *Integrity* Magazine [1950's] (Kansas City, MO: Angelus Press, 1999), pp. 41-43.
3. *Ibid.*
4. *Ibid.,* p. 42.
5. Chesterton, *op. cit.,* p. 87.
6. Alice von Hildebrand, op. cit., p. 37.
7. D. Q. McInerny, *A Course in Thomistic Ethics* (Elmhurst, PA: The Priestly Fraternity of St. Peter, 1997), p. 173.
8. St. Thomas Aquinas, *Summa Theologica*, I-II, Q. 61, art. 3, 4.
9. John Kamprath, Director of Professional Development for the National Association of Private Catholic and Independent Schools. More information and additional resources can be found at the Association's website http://www.napcis.org/

10. *Summa Theologica*, II-II, Q. 168, art. 1 ff.
11. Alice von Hildebrand, op. cit., p. 62.
12. *Ibid.,* p. 63.
13. *Ibid.*, p. 47.
14. Chesterton, *op. cit.*, p. 113, in von Hildebrand, *op. cit.*, p. 47.
15. Alice von Hildebrand, *op. cit.,* p. 37.
16. *Ibid.*, p. 44.
17. *Ibid.,* p. 45.
18. *Ibid.*
19. *Ibid.*, p. 10.
20. *Summa Theologica* (II, 169, 2) "Reply to Objection 3. As stated in the foregoing Article, outward apparel should be consistent with the estate of the person, according to the general custom. Hence it is in itself sinful for a woman to wear man's clothes, or vice versa; especially since this may be a cause of sensuous pleasure; and it is expressly forbidden in the Law (*Deut.* 22:5) because the Gentiles used to practice this change of attire for the purpose of idolatrous superstition. Nevertheless, this may be done sometimes without sin on account of some necessity, either in order to hide oneself from enemies, or through lack of other clothes, or for some similar motive."
21. Helen B. Andelin, *Fascinating Womanhood*, Updated Edition (Pacific Press, 1965; New York: Bantam Books, a division of Random House, 1992), pp. 248-249.
22. *Summa Theologica* (II-II, 169, 2) "Reply to Objection 2. Cyprian is speaking of women painting themselves: this is a kind of falsification, which cannot be devoid of sin. Wherefore Augustine says (*Ep. ccxlv ad Possid.*): 'To dye oneself with paints in order to have a rosier or a paler complexion is a lying counterfeit. I doubt whether even their husbands are willing to be deceived by it, by whom alone' (i.e., the husbands) 'are they to be permitted, but not ordered, to adorn themselves.' However, such painting does not always involve a mortal sin, but only when it is done for the sake of sensuous pleasure or in contempt of God, and it is to like cases that Cyprian refers. It must, however, be observed that it is one thing to counterfeit a beauty one has not, and another to hide a disfigurement arising from some cause such as sickness or the like. For this is lawful, since according to the Apostle (*1 Cor.* 12:23), 'such as we think to be the less honorable members of the body, about these we put more abundant honor.'"
23. Andelin, *op. cit.,* p. 255.
24. Cf. *ibid.*, p. 257.
25. *Ibid.*, pp. 263-264.
26. "Moral Problems in Fashion Design: Address of Pius XII to a Congress of the Latin Union of High Fashion," Nov. 8, 1957. www.sspxasia.com/Documents/CatholicMorality/Fashions.html
27. Pope Benedict XV, "Allocution to a Group of Italian Women," Oct. 21, 1919, in *WMW*, p. 32.

☙ CHAPTER SIX ❧

Outfit Guidelines

THERE is a difference between fashion and style. When you hear the word *fashion*, you probably think of a runway in Paris. If we say that someone is fashionable, we usually mean that she tries to keep up-to-date on current trends in clothing.

But what we're talking about here is *style*, which is a language all its own. What we wear speaks to those around us. And many times we don't realize the subconscious communication that goes on between our clothing and the people we are with. People do judge a book by its cover.

When I first came across this information about dressing in a tasteful, dignified and feminine manner, I didn't own a dress. My wardrobe consisted of T-shirts, sweats, jeans and a few blouses.

So I made a dress. It was too short. Let's just say it didn't fit the definition of "dignified." Because I thought being feminine meant wearing any ol' dress, I didn't realize that my lack of material was anything but dignified.

Then I ran across the Vatican's guidelines for modest dressing:

> . . . a dress cannot be called decent which is cut deeper than two fingers' breadth under the pit of the throat, which does not cover the arms at least to the elbows,* and scarcely reaches a bit beyond

---

* Short sleeves were also permitted as a temporary concession, with ecclesiastical approval, because of "impossible market conditions."

91

the knees. Furthermore, dresses of transparent material are improper.[1]

You know, I have yet to meet a person who doesn't agree that these guidelines are completely reasonable! I agree. Plus, I like the fact that they give me something concrete to go on!

As the saying goes, there is a difference between dressing attractively and dressing to attract. Modesty is not just about how much skin is showing, but also about how much of our feminine form is showing.[2] But that doesn't mean we must go around looking frumpy and wearing tents or potato sacks . . . or clothing that looks like them. Women should adorn themselves moderately, but not excessively, shamelessly or immodestly.[3]

Dressing tastefully begins with using the Blessed Virgin Mary as our example.

If you look at the major approved Marian apparitions, or at a statue of our Blessed Mother, you will get an idea of what feminine dressing is all about.

At Guadalupe, Mexico in 1531, the Blessed Mother left a self-portrait on St. Juan Diego's cloak, which has been miraculously preserved for nearly five centuries. The image shows her wearing a pink gown, beautifully embroidered, with a blue mantle covered with stars and a sash around her waist.

An angel woke up young Sister Catherine Labouré one night in 1830 at her convent in Paris and led her to the chapel. Sister Catherine heard the sound of rustling silk, which was followed by an appearance of Our Lady. Later, our Blessed Mother gave her a vision of the Miraculous Medal that she wanted struck. On it, Mary is wearing a long, flowing gown with a belt around her waist and a long veil or mantle over her head.

Melanie and Maximin, the two children privileged to see Our Lady in 1846 at La Salette, France, described her as very tall and beautiful, wearing a long, white, pearl-studded, long-sleeved dress, with a white shawl, some sort of belt and a crown on her head.

In 1858, at Lourdes, France, fourteen-year-old St. Bernadette Soubirous described how she had seen Mary clothed in a brilliant and unearthly white robe, with a blue sash around her waist and a white veil on her head. Our Lady of Lourdes also had a golden rose on each of her feet and a rosary over her arm.

Four young children in Pontmain, France, saw our Blessed Mother in 1871. They said she was wearing a blue gown covered with golden stars, a short red cross over her heart and a black veil under a golden crown.[4]

Fifteen villagers in Knock, Ireland saw the Blessed Virgin Mary, St. Joseph and St. John the Evangelist in 1879. In that apparition Mary was wearing "a long gown and a crown of pulsating brilliance, with a golden rose over her forehead."[5]

In 1917, Our Lady appeared to Lucia dos Santos and her two cousins, Francisco and Jacinta Marto in Fatima, Portugal. Lucia described her as a lady clothed in white, brighter than the sun, radiating a light clearer and more intense than a crystal cup filled with sparkling water lit by burning sunlight, and wearing a mantle that was trimmed in elaborate gold.

Between November 1932 and January 1933, five children in Beauraing, Belgium saw our Blessed Mother, whom they described as wearing a white, luminous, long and flowing gown, walking in mid-air, with her feet hidden by a little cloud.

Early in 1933, Mariette Beco of Banneux, Belgium had a vision of Mary; our Blessed Mother was wearing a long white gown with a blue belt, as well as a transparent white veil on her head.

These appearances occurred over a period of more than four centuries, but did you notice how Mary is dressed basically the same? She is wearing graceful, feminine and flowing dresses. But there is something else. She is usually described as having a sash or a belt around her waist.

What is it that defines a woman? Her bust and her hips are larger than her waist. A belt or sash defines that feature, but doesn't cause the garment to cling to the body.

Of course, I'm not suggesting we all go out and purchase long flowing gowns with a blue sash like Mary. Besides, for most of us, money is tight. Very few women have a budget large enough to go out right now and replace all the clothing they have in their closets.

But there are some fashion tricks you can use to make your present wardrobe both fashionable, feminine and dignified—if it isn't already. Even if you do have the money in your budget to replace some of the less dignified fashions in your closet, with the limited availability of tasteful fashions today, your options are restricted. You can, however, find clothing in your local stores that will be fashionable and still clothe your body in a modest and dignified manner. (A resale shop may actually offer a better variety of styles than many stores.) Rome has given us the general guidelines, but it sure is helpful to have some specifics to look for when we shop.

I have become acquainted with Dannah Gresh, a modesty and chastity speaker and the author of *Secret Keeper: The Delicate Power of Modesty,* who has been seen on the Christian Broadcast Network. The outfit guidelines that follow are based on Dannah's Modesty Tests,[6] with her permission.

Let's Start with the Top

Is the blouse, shirt or top well designed? When shopping for a top, here are a few tips to keep in mind:

First, try it on in front of a mirror and bend over. How far does the neckline drop away from your chest? Can you see down your top to your chest? Or, worse yet, your belly button? If you can see down your shirt, then so can everyone else.

Fashion Tip: Do you have a shirt (or two) like this in your closet? This is easy to remedy! Wearing a camisole or T-shirt underneath this shirt will solve this problem. Also, an oblong scarf will fix the shirt so that you can wear it with comfort once again. Here is a fashionable idea that I learned in Paris a couple of years ago.

Take a scarf (approximately 5 to 6 feet long and 4 to 12 inches wide) and fold it in half lengthwise over your left wrist. With your right hand, grab the bottom of the two ends of the scarf. Hold the scarf horizontally in front of you. Now you have the scarf looped over your left wrist and stretched over to your right hand. Keeping the scarf grasped in your right hand and looped over your left wrist, place the folded scarf across the back of your neck. Still keeping the scarf looped over your left wrist, take your left hand and reach around the front of your throat. Grab the tail ends of the scarf that you are holding in your right hand. Now, pull the tail ends of the scarf through the loop that you have over your left wrist. *Voila!* This is an instant fix for your baggy-blouse dilemma. You can now wear your blouse and not worry about what may be seen when you bend over.

Second, when wearing a knit shirt, take your fingertips and press them into your shirt over your breastbone. When you take your hand away, does the shirt immediately spring back? If so, the shirt doesn't work because it is too tight. (Well-endowed ladies need to be extra careful!)

Fashion Tip: Sorry, no fashion tips for this one. Get rid of this too-tight shirt.

Third, does the shirt button down the front? Stand sideways to the mirror and put your hands on your hips (like "chicken wings"). Now try to touch your elbows together behind your back. If the shirt is tight enough to cause a gap, you're in danger of exposing too much—not to mention being in danger of losing a button and exposing even more!

Fashion Tip: Blouses and shirts that are too tight are unbecoming, especially for a lady who dresses with dignity. Ignore the "size" number, and go for a size or two larger to allow the shirt to be looser, and for you to be able to move freely. You can also wear a camisole (or if you can't afford one right now, try a T-shirt) under the shirt. It's important to make sure the camisole or T-shirt also passes the modesty test!

Fourth, does your neckline plunge down too low in the front? A shirt is not attractive or demure if it dips lower than two fingers' width below your collarbone. The shirt should also have sleeves that cover your shoulders and upper arms. Oh, and also make sure you're not exposing your upper back.

Fashion Tip: Just like with the baggy shirt above, use an oblong fashion scarf. It will fill in the area below your collarbone left exposed by your shirt.

Fifth, reach up as if you're getting something off the top shelf. Does that expose any back or belly skin? If so, then this shirt doesn't work because it is too short.

Fashion Tip: Pull out that camisole again!

Finally, does the top have any type of writing or message on it? A confident lady has the good taste not to use her bosom as a billboard. A top with a message doesn't work. Ditch it.

Dresses and Skirts

How long? How short? Let's just use the Vatican guidelines (see pp. 91-92), which in practice would translate to about "two inches below the knee." (Or go with Padre Pio's requirement of eight inches below the knee!) Remember to check for coverage when sitting with your legs crossed too.

Does the skirt or dress have slits? Forget it! It's better to forego altogether a skirt or dress with slits. If an outfit has a slit in it for "ease of movement," then it's probably too tight for comfort . . . or elegance! And even if a slit goes only a short way up the skirt, it still attracts men's eyes to your legs, which frustrates your efforts to be modest. Unless you can sew them up, slits are definitely out!

Fashion Tip: You can find long, flowing skirts almost anywhere today. A dignified lady keeps her kneecaps covered . . . even when she's sitting. And don't forget to wear a slip!

Tight, Clingy, Sheer

Can you see your undergarments, or undergarment lines?

As mentioned earlier, dressing with dignity is about more than how much of our skin is showing . . . it's also about how much of our feminine form is revealed.

Before you purchase something (or leave the house), take a good look at your outfit in a full-length mirror and look for these things:

How tight is it? Can you see any undergarment lines because of the outer clothing being too snug?

How clingy is it? When you move around, does the garment flow freely away from your body, or does it cling and show your bra and panty lines, or too much of your feminine form?

How transparent is it? Can you see your bra or panties through the material?

Does any portion of your undergarments poke out from underneath your clothing and become visible for all to see?

If you can see an outline of your undergarments, then that item of clothing is too tight, too clingy, or too sheer.

Fashion Tip: Trash any clothing that is tight, clingy, or transparent. It's immodest, undignified and just plain in bad taste.

"Head, Shoulders, Knees and Toes"

My grandmother taught me a little ditty when I was a child, and I've passed it along to my daughter: "Head, shoulders, knees and toes!" My daughter added a second line and made it a poem. Before we buy anything, she says:

> "Head, shoulders, knees and toes.
> Doesn't work?
> Then out it goes!"

How can you apply this?

1. Put your hands on your *head*. Does the skin around your waist show (stomach or back)?
2. Put your hands on your *shoulders*. Are your shoulders still covered? Check your neckline, too, and make sure it isn't too low.
3. Bend over and put your hands on your *knees*. Does your dress or shirt hang open and away from your body? (This needs to be fixed, or change the garment!) Does your clothing cover your knees? If so, then you probably don't have to worry about showing something you don't want to.
4. Bend down and touch your *toes*. Does your back show?

If you can pass the head-shoulders-knees-and-toes test, congratulations! You are now developing a style all your own—and dressing with dignity!

NOTES

1. Issued by the Cardinal Vicar of Pope Pius XI in Rome, September 24, 1928, in "Rome's Decrees . . .," *op. cit.* (cf. note 37, p. 73 above).
2. "Truth or Bare" Modesty Tests. www.purefreedom.org
3. *Summa Theologica* (II-II, Q. 169, art. 2) "Reply to Objection 1. As a gloss says on this passage, 'The wives of those who were in distress despised their husbands, and decked themselves that they might please other men': and the Apostle forbids this. Cyprian is speaking in the same sense; yet he does not forbid married women to adorn themselves in order to please their husbands, lest the latter be afforded an occasion of sin with other women. Hence the Apostle says (*1 Tim.* 2:9): 'Women . . . in ornate [Douay: "decent"] apparel, adorning themselves with modesty and sobriety, not with plaited hair, or gold, or pearls, or costly attire': whence we are given to understand that sober and moderate adornment is not forbidden for women; but rather, excessive, shameless and immodest adornment."
4. www.ourladyofhope.net
5. Rev. Paul E. Duggan, *The Priest* (Huntington, IN: Our Sunday Visitor Publishing, 1999). www.catholicculture.org
6. www.purefreedom.org/magazine/truth_or_bare.html

CHAPTER SEVEN

What's Next

WHAT I have tried to do in this book is provide you with information that will help you see the immense privilege of your femininity. I've also tried to give some suggestions and guidelines for you to find your own deeply embedded womanhood, polish it up, and bring it to the forefront.

By the time I started researching fashion history and the Church documents to write this book, I considered myself a very modest dresser. But necklines that were slightly too low, sleeveless dresses (it gets mighty hot here in Texas!) and slits to above my knees were my downfall. But, when I decided to change, I figured if the hundreds of generations of women before me could dress with modesty and dignity, so could I!

I'm over six feet tall, so finding long enough skirts and sleeves that reach my elbows is sometimes a challenge. But if I can dress according to the "Outfit Guidelines," I think it's fair to say that pretty much anyone else can too.

Changing to a more modest way of dressing did not come easily for me, and it may not for you either. But conforming ourselves to what is right rarely does! Believe me, it was hard enough just confronting the information I found about how women should dress and why. The more I progressed through my research for this book, the more upset I became. Then I became horrified. Let's face it . . . . *this information is radical and counter-cultural to just about everything we encounter today in female fashions!* I'm sure that's just how Satan wants it to be. He knows how many people fall away when the going gets tough. And like me, you too may find yourself forced to make a decision as to what is best for you and your children in the eyes of God. That decision may or may not come easily, but it is yours to make!

Fortunately, today we can say that there is a trend beginning out there regarding the fashion choices available to us.

Eleven-year-old Ella Gunderson made news in the Seattle area, and then nationally, when her letter to Nordstrom came to the attention of company executives. Ella wrote:

> Dear Nordstrom,
> I'm an 11-year-old girl who has tried shopping at your store for clothes, in particular jeans, but all of them ride way under my hips, and the next size up is too big and falls down. They're also way too tight, and as I get older, show everything every time I move. I see all of these girls who walk around with pants that show their belly button and underwear. Even at my age, I know that that is not modest. With a pair of clothes from your store, I'd walk around showing half of my body and not fully dressed. Your clerk suggested there is only one look. If that is true, then girls are supposed to walk around half-naked. I think maybe you should change that.[1]

Two Nordstrom executives responded with letters promising to work on more fashion choices for customers. One store manager wrote back:

> Wow, your letter really got my attention . . . I think you are absolutely right. There should not be just one look for everyone. This look is not particularly a modest one and there should be choices for everyone.[2]

Ella's mother commented, "The girls want to look feminine and they want to look pretty, but the only look the stores offer is sexy."[3] Miss Gunderson, a number of mothers and 37 other girls from Holy Family School went ahead and put together their own "Pure Fashion" show at a Hyatt Regency. (A photo of Ella modeling a skirt and top outfit is featured with the online news story.) The sold-out event even received donations of modest clothing from local stores.[4]

Another fashion victory came when Dillard's in Tucson took note of young customers' wishes—expressed in a petition drive—and decided to offer more modest fashion choices. The petition asked for clothing that "covers the midriff, bust, shoulders, back, legs to the knees—in general, clothing that shows respect for the body."[5] In particular, Dillard's decided to send its Tucson stores more modest jeans and prom dresses.[6]

In one department store I know of, employees jokingly refer to immodest fashions as "floozywear"! It's nice to see mainstream society recognizing that much of the stuff available in the stores is inappropriate.

I have been speaking to many gatherings of women and girls in various parts of the country regarding modest, dignified, feminine dress. These presentations usually feature a fashion show. It is extremely encouraging to be a part of such a wonderful movement toward dressing with dignity. Let's keep it up!

When you live your femininity devotedly, you will see people around you change the way they respond to you. You may be reluctant to practice walking with a book on your head. You may feel silly learning to laugh in a more feminine manner. But you will find that when you relinquish all masculine characteristics that you may have picked up and then intensify your femininity, you will be amply rewarded with what might be for you a whole new—and pleasantly natural—outlook on life. And also you will begin to see your life through the eyes of a woman, a real honest-to-goodness woman who is your real self, as *God* created you to be!

We can change the world—one outfit at a time!

This said, I want to hear from you! The information you share will help me to edit and expand future editions of *Dressing with Dignity*.

Think back through the book. If you've decided to make any changes in the way you dress, please let me know what information helped *you* make that choice. What changes have you made in the way you dress, in your mannerisms? What haven't you changed? Do you think you ever will?

A tremendous encouragement for me is hearing success stories of other women. As you grow in your God-given femininity, I am confident that He will reward you with a richer, fuller, more feminine life. Please drop me a note and tell me your personal story.

I look forward to hearing from you!

NOTES

1. Michelle Malkin, "Decency takes a stand: Modesty in a culture of excess," *The Washington Times*, August 9-15, 2004, p. 4.
2. Nick Perry, "More modest clothing, please, girl asks Nordstrom," *The Seattle Times*, Local News, May 21, 2004. http://seattle times.nwsource.com/html/localnews/2001934910_fash. . .
3. *Ibid.*
4. Malkin, *op. cit.,* p. 4.
5. Scott Simonson, "Local teens score one for modesty," *Arizona Daily Star*, Section: News, Sept. 18, 2004. http://www.dailystar.com/dailystar/dailystar/39487.php
6. *Ibid.*

Appendices

∽ Appendix One ∾

Addresses of Websites

LISTED here are addresses of various websites where you can find modest clothing. My biggest regret is that the availability of clothing that is modest, feminine *and* chic is so drastically limited. It is my wish that our *Petition to Clothing Manufacturers* will change all of that. (Please sign the Petition on my website!)[1] (If I had time, I'd like to develop my own line of clothing!)

These websites are from a wide variety of sources. A few are Catholic, some are secular, some are sites of other religions—and not all the clothing on each website will pass the Outfit Guidelines, either!

Some websites are small cottage businesses, some are large companies, and some are seamstresses that make outfits to your specifications.

A few of these sites offer clothing that some may consider "hip" or "chic." The rest handle a more "classic" look.

Check my website for additional resources because I will be posting more as I find them. And if you have a business that you would like to see listed, please email me and give me the URL.

Use your discretion and common sense when visiting each site and selecting clothing for your family. I offer these websites only as a service. *I do not guarantee the sites, nor do I promise anything about them,*

---

1. www.ColleenHammond.com

endorse them, or recommend any one website or business over another.

Caveat Emptor—"Let the buyer beware!"

Note: If you don't have access to the internet, visit or
call the Reference Desk at your local public library
and ask if a librarian would print out the phone number and/or postal address of sites in which you have
a particular interest.

Women and/or Girls Everyday Wear
Hannah Lise www.hannahlise.com/
Little Touch of Elegance
   www.littletouchofelegance.com
Made with Love www.madewithtlc.com
Modest Apparel USA
   www.modestapparelusa.com/
Simply Skirts
   www.simplyskirts.com/pages/1/index.html
Modest By Design
   www.modestbydesign.com/Home
Cattle Kate www.cattlekate.com
Strasburg Children www.strasburgchildren.com
Storybook Heirlooms www.storybook.com
Anna Bouché Designer Children's Clothing
   www.annabouche.com
Melody Children's Clothing www.melodyclothing.com
French Toast www.frenchtoast.com
Great Lengths www.greatlengths.com
4 Modesty www.4modesty.com/
Recollections www.recollections.biz
ModesTee www.makeitmodest.com/
Lilies of the Field www.liliesapparel.com/
Seams like Yesterday www.seamslikeyesterday.com
Baker Lane www.bakerlane.com/
Ringger Clothing www.ringgerclothing.com
Cottage Primrose www.cottageprimrose.com

Vessels of Mercy
   www.finitesite.com/vesselsofmercy/
Sweet Marie's Modest Dresses
   www.sweetmariesmodestdresses.com/
Hausmutti's Modest Dresses
   www.hausmutti.com/
Marylike Modesty www.marylikemodesty.com
Works of the Heart
   www.worksoftheheart.com/index.html
Emme's Garden www.emmesgarden.com/
Designs by Lynda
   www.modest-clothing.com/index.html
The Prairie Closet www.prairiecloset.com
Wardrobe Classics www.wardrobeclassics.com/
She Maketh Herself Coverings (includes skirts)
   www.headcoverings.com/
Practically Pretty by Design
   www.practicallyprettydesign.com
Pure in Heart www.pureinheart.hypermart.net/
Inspired Threads
   www.inspiredthreads.com
The King's Daughters
   www.thekingsdaughters.com/
Lydia of Purple   www.lydiaofpurple.com

Mainstream Retailers
Orvis www.orvis.com
Blair www.blair.com
Travelsmith www.travelsmith.com
Appleseed's www.appleseeds.com
Land's End www.landsend.com
April Cornell www.aprilcornell.com
The Vermont Country Store
   www.vermontcountrystore.com
Maryland Square www.marylandsquare.com

Veils
Modesty Veils www.modestyveils.com/
Halo Works www.halo-works.com/
Immaculate Heart Mantillas
    www.lffa-ollmpc.com/ihm/index.html
She Maketh Herself Coverings
    www.headcoverings.com/

Patterns
Baker Lane www.bakerlane.com/
Sense and Sensibility www.sensibility.com/
Kathy's Modest Patterns
    www.modestpatterns.com/
Harper House www.longago.com/
FREE Period Patterns
    www.tudorlinks.com/treasury/freepatterns/
Birch Street Folkwear www.birchstreet.folkwear.com
Elizabeth Lee Designs (For Breastfeeding Moms)
    www.elizabethlee.com
Swimwear Solutions
    www.freewebs.com/swimwear_solutions/

Swimwear
Little Touch of Elegance
    www.littletouchofelegance.com/
Swim Modest www.swimmodest.com
SolarTex www.solartex.com/Detail.bok?no=26
Swimwear Solutions
    www.freewebs.com/swimwear_solutions/
WholesomeWear www.wholesomewear.com/
Lilies of the Field www.liliesapparel.com

Formal (*Note: Most of the modest bridal/prom
  sites on the internet seem to be run by Mormons.*)
Simply Elegant www.simplyelegantforyou.com
Eternity Gowns www.eternitygowns.com/
LDS* Brides www.ldsbrides.com/
Beautifully Modest Formal Wear
  www.beautifullymodest.com/index.html
Kathleen's Bridal (Mormon)
  www.Kathleensbridal.com
Lynette's www.lynettes.com
Modest Prom
  www.modestprom.com/gownideas/
Great Lengths www.greatlengths.com/

Men
Knee Shorts www.kneeshorts.com/
Great Lengths www.greatlengths.com/

Practical Tips
"Wearing Dresses Gracefully," article by Mrs. Stanley
  Sherman, illustrated with photos of Rebecca
  Newton of Baker Lane. October 2004.
www.ladiesagainstfeminism.org/artman/publish/
  article_1403.shtml

"Through the Week in Feminine Dress," article by
  Mrs. Jennie Chancey, with photos. April 2002.
www.ladiesagainstfeminism.com/articles/
  weekinfemininedress/mrschancey.htm

"Getting Used to Dresses," by Mrs. Stanley Sherman,
  with photos. December 2003.
www.ladiesagainstfeminism.com/artman/publish/
  article_649.shtml

---

* LDS stands for Latter Day Saints (Mormon).

"How to Dress Modestly in a Modern World," by
   Carolyn Moir. October 2003.
www.ladiesagainstfeminism.com/artman/publish/
   article_567.shtml

"Dressing Little Girls," by Tonya Davis. January 2004.
www.ladiesagainstfeminism.com/artman/publish/
   article_714.shtml

Quotes from Scripture, Saints, Popes, Private Revelation

Holy Scripture

"A woman shall not be clothed with man's apparel, neither shall a man use woman's apparel: for he that does these things is abominable before God."

—*Deuteronomy* 22:5

"I made a covenant with my eyes, that I would not so much as think upon a virgin."　　—*Job* 31:1

"The queen stood on thy right hand, in gilded clothing; surrounded with variety."　　—*Psalm* 44:10

"You have heard that it was said to the ancients, 'Thou shall not commit adultery.' But I say to you that anyone who so much as looks with lust at a woman has already committed adultery with her in his heart. And if thy right eye scandalize thee, pluck it out and cast it from thee. For it is expedient for thee that one of thy members should perish, rather than that thy whole body be cast into hell."　　—*Matthew* 5:27-29

"For know you this and understand, that no fornicator, or unclean, or covetous person (which is serving of idols), hath inheritance in the kingdom of Christ and of God. Let no man deceive you with vain words. For because of these things cometh the anger of God upon the children of unbelief. Be ye not therefore partakers with them. For you were heretofore darkness, but now light in the Lord. Walk then as children of the light."   —*Ephesians* 5:5-8

"Know you not, that you are the temple of God, and that the Spirit of God dwelleth in you? But if any man violate the temple of God, him shall God destroy. For the temple of God is holy, which you are."
                          —*1 Corinthians* 3:16-17

"But every woman praying or prophesying with her head not covered, disgraceth her head: for it is all one as if she were shaven. For if a woman be not covered, let her be shorn. But if it be a shame to a woman to be shorn or made bald, let her cover her head. . . . Therefore ought the woman to have a power over her head, because of the angels. . . . You yourselves judge: doth it become a woman, to pray unto God uncovered? . . ."   —*1 Corinthians* 11:5-15

"But the fruit of the Spirit is, charity, joy, peace, patience, benignity, goodness, longanimity, mildness, faith, modesty, continency, chastity."
                              —*Galatians* 5:22-23

"In like manner women also in decent apparel: adorning themselves with modesty and sobriety, not with plaited hair, or gold, or pearls, or costly attire, but as it becometh women professing godliness, with good works."   —*1 Timothy* 2:9-10

Saints

St. John Chrysostom (347-407)
"You carry your snare everywhere and spread your nets in all places. You allege that you never invited others to sin. You did not, indeed, by your words, but

you have done so by your dress and your deportment. . . . When you have made another sin in his heart, how can you be innocent? Tell me, whom does this world condemn? Whom do judges punish? Those who drink poison or those who prepare it and administer the fatal potion? You have prepared the abominable cup, you have given the death-dealing drink, and you are more criminal than are those who poison the body; you murder not the body but the soul. And it is not to enemies you do this, nor are you urged on by any imaginary necessity, nor provoked by injury, but out of foolish vanity and pride." —St. John Chrysostom, Archbishop of Constantinople, Doctor of the Church, and one of the Four Great Eastern Fathers of the Church.

St. John Vianney (1786-1859)

"There are mothers who have so little religion or, if you like, are so ignorant, that if they want to show off their baby to some neighboring mothers, they will show it to them naked. Others, when they are putting on diapers, will leave the babies, for a long period of time, uncovered before everyone. Now even if there is no one present at all, you should not do this. Should you not respect the presence of their Guardian Angels? . . ." —*Sermons of the Curé of Ars*, Impr., TAN, 1995, p. 82.

Bl. Jacinta Marto (1908-1919), one of the three seers at Fatima, Portugal in 1917

"Certain fashions will be introduced which will offend Our Lord very much. Persons who serve God must not follow the fashions. The Church does not have fashions; Our Lord is always the same. The sins of the world are very great. . . ." —Cf. *A Flower of Fatima*, by Reverend Galamba de Oliveira, Imprimatur, DSP, Boston, c. 1959, p. 164.

"Some days, Jacinta while in the hospital was very saddened by the worldliness of the visitors, the women dressed in fashionable clothes, often with low-cut dresses. 'What is it all for?' she asked Mother Godinho (her guardian). 'If they only knew what eternity is.'"

Alexandrina da Costa (1904-1955)

"Vanity and extravagance in the world must cease." "Let those exhibiting their bodies clothe themselves. Let modesty reign. Penance! Prayer! Much prayer is needed!" (Words of Our Lord to Alexandrina).
—*Alexandrina*, by Francis Johnston, Imprimatur, TAN, 1982, p. 101.

St. Padre Pio of Pietrelcina (1887-1968), Priest, mystic, stigmatist and director of souls

"Padre Pio wouldn't tolerate low-necked dresses or short, tight skirts, and he forbade his spiritual daughters to wear transparent stockings. Each year his severity increased. He stubbornly dismissed them from his confessional, even before they set foot inside, if he judged them to be improperly dressed. On some mornings he drove away one after another, until he ended up hearing very few Confessions.

"His brothers observed these drastic purges with a certain uneasiness and decided to fasten a sign on the church door: 'By Padre Pio's explicit wish, women must enter his confessional wearing skirts at least eight inches below the knees. It is forbidden to borrow longer dresses in church and to wear them for the confessional.'" —*Prophet of the People*, by Dorothy M. Gaudiose, Impr., Alba House, Staten Island, 1974, p. 191.

Popes

Pope Benedict XV (1914-1922)

"This point, We feel, must be particularly stressed. For, on the one hand, We know that certain modes of dress which women are beginning to accept, are harmful to society, for they are a cause of evil. And on the other hand, We find, to our amazement, that those who spread this poison seem to ignore its evil effects: those who set the house on fire, as it were, seem not to realize the destructive power of the flames. And yet only such an ignorance can explain the deplorable popularity of fashions so contrary to that sense of modesty which should be the most beautiful adornment of the Christian woman. If she realized what she was doing, woman would hardly go so far as to enter the church indecently clad, to appear before those who are the natural and authorized teachers in matters of Christian morality." —Pope Benedict XV, from "Allocution to a group of Italian women," October 21, 1919 (*WMW*, p. 29).

1928 Letter of the Sacred Congregation for Religious under Pope Pius XI

"In order to confront a danger which, by spreading, becomes ever more grave, this Sacred Congregation, by order of the Holy Father [Pope Pius XI], calls upon the Ordinaries [bishops] of Italy so that they may communicate to the superiors of the houses of female religious in their respective dioceses the following injunctions of this Sacred Congregation, confirmed by His Holiness in audience this day:

"a) In all schools, academies, recreation centers, Sunday schools, and laboratories directed by female religious, not to be admitted from now on are those girls who do not observe in their attire the rules of modesty and Christian decency.

"b) To this end, the superiors themselves will be obliged to exercise a close supervision and exclude peremptorily from the schools and projects of their institutions those pupils who do not conform to these prescriptions.

"c) They must not be influenced in this by any human

respect, either for material considerations or by reason of the social prestige of the families of their pupils, even though the student body should diminish in number.

"d) Furthermore, the Sisters, in fulfillment of their educational pursuits, must endeavor to inculcate sweetly and strongly in their pupils the love and relish for holy modesty, the sign and guardian of purity and delicate adornment of womankind. . . ."

Devotedly yours,
G. Cardinal Laurenti, Prefect
(of Sac. Congr. for Relig.)
Vincent La Puma, Secretary
Rome, August 23, 1928

—Excerpts from the 1928 Letter of the Sacred Congregation for Religious to the Ordinaries of Italy (*Acta Apostolicae Sedis*, 1930, Vol. 22, pp. 26-28).

The "Vatican Guidelines"

"We recall that a dress cannot be called decent which is cut deeper than two fingers' breadth under the pit of the throat, which does not cover the arms at least to the elbows,* and scarcely reaches a bit beyond the knees. Furthermore, dresses of transparent material are improper . . ."

—Issued by the Cardinal Vicar (Basilio Pompili) of Pope Pius XI in Rome, September 24, 1928.

1930 Letter of the Sacred Congregation of the Council under Pope Pius XI

"Very often, when occasion arose, the same Supreme Pontiff [Pope Pius XI] condemned emphatically the immodest fashion of dress adopted by Catholic women and girls, which fashion not only offends the dignity

---

* Short sleeves were also permitted as a temporary concession, with ecclesiastical approval, because of "impossible market conditions."

of women and against her adornment, but conduces to the temporal ruin of the women and girls, and, what is still worse, to their eternal ruin, miserably dragging down others in their fall. . . .

"In order to facilitate the desired effect, this Sacred Congregation, by the mandate of the Most Holy Father [Pope Pius XI], has decreed as follows:

"1. The parish priest, and especially the preacher, when occasion arises, should, according to the words of the Apostle Paul (*2 Tim.* 4:2), insist, argue, exhort and command that feminine garb be based on modesty, and womanly ornament be a defense of virtue. Let them likewise admonish parents to cause their daughters to cease wearing indecorous dress. . . .

"2. Parents, conscious of their grave obligations toward the education, especially religious and moral, of their offspring, should see to it that their daughters are solidly instructed, from earliest childhood, in Christian doctrine; and they themselves should assiduously inculcate in their souls, by word and example, love for the virtues of modesty and chastity. . . .

"3. Let parents keep their daughters away from public gymnastic games and contests; but if their daughters are compelled to attend such exhibitions, let them see that they are fully and modestly dressed. Let them never permit their daughters to don immodest garb. . . .

"7. It is desirable that pious organizations of women be founded, which by their counsel, example and propaganda should combat the wearing of apparel unsuited to Christian modesty, and should promote purity of customs and modesty of dress. . . .

"9. Maidens and women dressed immodestly are to be debarred from Holy Communion and from acting as sponsors at the Sacraments of Baptism and Confirmation; further, if the offense be extreme, they may even be forbidden to enter the church."

—Donato, Cardinal Sbaretti
(Prefect of Cong. of Council)
Rome, January 12, 1930.
—Excerpts from 1930 Letter of the Sacred Congregation of the Council [now called the Sacred Congregra-
tion for the Clergy] to the world (*Acta Apostolicae Sedis*,
1930, Vol. 22).

Pope Pius XII (1939-1958)

"Conscience and grace, which do not destroy nature
but perfect it, place in the soul, as it were, a sense
which renders it vigilant against the dangers threatening purity. This is especially a characteristic of the
young Christian girl. We read in the *Passion of Sts.
Perpetua and Felicity*—rightly regarded as one of the
most precious gems of early Christian literature—that
in the amphitheatre at Carthage, when the martyr
Vibia Perpetua, thrown high into the air by a savage
cow, fell to the ground, her first thought and action
was to rearrange her dress to cover her thigh, because
she was more concerned for modesty than pain. . . .

"Many women . . . have forgotten Christian modesty
because of vanity and ambition: they rush wretchedly
into dangers which can spell death to their purity. They
give in to the tyranny of fashion, be it even immodest, in such a way as to appear not even to suspect
that it is unbecoming. They have lost the very concept
of danger: they have lost the instinct of modesty."
—Pope Pius XII, from "Allocution to the Girls of Catholic
Action," October 6, 1940. (*WMW*, p. 51).

Pope Pius XII (1939-1958)

"Some young ladies may remark that a certain form
of dress is more convenient, or even more hygienic;
but if it becomes a grave and proximate danger for the
soul, it is certainly not hygienic for the spirit, and you
must reject it. The salvation of their souls made hero-

ines of the martyrs, like the Agneses and the Cecilias, amidst the sufferings and tortures of their virginal bodies: and will you, their sisters in the Faith, in the love of Christ, in the esteem for virtue, not find at the bottom of your hearts the courage and strength to sacrifice a little well-being—a physical advantage, if you like—to conserve safe and pure the life of your souls? And if, simply for one's own pleasure, one has not the right to endanger the physical health of others, is it not still less licit to compromise the health, or rather the very life, of their souls?

"If, as some women say, a bold fashion does not leave them with any evil impressions, how can they know anything of the impression made on others? Who can assure them that others do not draw therefrom incentives to evil? You do not know the depths of human frailty, nor what blood drips from the wounds left by Adam's sin in human nature, with its ignorance in the intellect, its malice in the will, its ardent desire of pleasure, and its weakness towards the perilous attractions of the passions of the sense; and this to such a degree that man, as receptive as wax to evil, 'sees what is better, and chooses what is worse,' because of that weight which always, like lead, drags him down to the depths.

"Oh, how truly was it said that if some Christian women could only suspect the temptations and falls they cause in others with modes of dress and familiarity in behaviour, which they unthinkingly consider as of no importance, they would be shocked by the responsibility which is theirs.

"And We do not hesitate to add:

"O Christian mothers, if you only knew what a future of worries and dangers, of ill subdued doubts, of hardly suppressed shame you lay up for your sons and your daughters by imprudently accostuming them to live barely attired, making them lose the natural sense of modesty, you yourselves would blush, and take fright at the shame you inflict upon yourselves, and the harm which you occasion to your children, entrusted to you by Heaven to be brought up in a Christian manner.

"And what We say to mothers, We repeat to many women among the faithful, and pious women at that, who, by showing their approval of this or that fashion, by their example lay low the last barriers which hold back from that fashion a mass of their sisters, for whom it may be a source of spiritual ruin. As long as certain audacious modes of dress remain the sad privilege of women of dubious reputation and almost a sign by which they may be known, no one else would dare to wear that same dress herself: but the moment that it appears upon persons beyond all reproach, she will hesitate no longer to follow the current, a current which will drag her perhaps to the worst falls."
—Pope Pius XII, from "Allocution to the Girls of Catholic Action," May 22, 1941. (*WMW*, p. 59-61).

Pope Pius XII (1939-1958)

"Therefore, train young Catholic women in that sublime and holy dignity which is so clear and powerful a safeguard of physical and spiritual integrity. This virtuous and indomitable stateliness and pride are a great ornament of the soul which will not be reduced to slavery. It enriches the moral vigor of the woman, who gives herself untouched only to her spouse, for the founding of a family, or else to God. It proclaims that her boast and glory is her vocation to the supernatural life and to eternity, just as St. Paul wrote to the early Christians: 'You have been bought at a great price. Glorify God and bear Him in your body.'

"The dignity and liberty of the woman who will not allow herself to be enslaved, even by fashion! This is a delicate but important question, in which your unceasing action permits us to hope for advantageous gains. Your zeal, however, against immodest forms of dress and behavior must be not only destructive, but also constructive, by showing in practice how a young woman can in her dress and deportment harmonize the higher laws of virtue and the norms of health and elegance."—Pope Pius XII, from "Allocution to the Girls of Catholic Action," April 24, 1943. (*WMW*, p. 115).

Pope Pius XII (1939-1958)

"Clothing, moreover, visibly and in a permanent way expresses the position of a person. This varies according to sex, age and social function. It shows both those things which link the individual with certain social classes and which, within those groups themselves, confer a special rank upon him. Formal clothes especially aim at making visible through the richness of their materials and their irreproachable tailoring the excellence of him who wears them." —Pope Pius XII, From "Allocution to the International Congress of Master Tailors," September 10, 1954. (*WMW*, p. 230).

"Mainly through sins of impurity do the forces of darkness subjugate souls."   —Pope Pius XII

"As long as modesty will not be put into practice, the society will continue to degrade. Society reveals what it is by the clothes it wears."   —Pope Pius XII

"To say that 'modesty is a matter of custom' is just as wrong as to say that 'honesty is a matter of custom.'"   —Pope Pius XII

Cardinal Pla y Daniel

"A special danger to morals is represented by public bathing at beaches . . . Mixed bathing between men and women, which is nearly always a proximate occasion of sin and a scandal, must be avoided." —Cardinal Pla y Daniel, Archbishop of Toledo, Spain, 1959.

Private Revelation

Our Lady of Good Fortune

"At the end of the 19th century and for a large part of the 20th, various heresies will flourish on this earth, which will have become a free republic. The precious light of the Faith will go out in souls because of the almost total moral corruption: in those times there will be great physical and moral calamities, in private and in public. The little number of souls keeping the Faith and practicing the virtues will undergo cruel and unspeakable suffering; through their long, drawn-out martyrdom, many of them will go to their death because of the violence of their sufferings, and those will count as martyrs who gave their lives for Church or for country.

"To escape from being enslaved by these heresies will call for great strength of will, constancy, courage, and great trust in God. . . .

". . . in those times, the air will be filled with the spirit of impurity, which, like a deluge of filth, will flood the streets, squares and public places. The licentiousness will be such that there will be no more virgin souls in the world.

". . . by having gained control of all the social classes, the sects will tend to penetrate with great skill into the hearts of families to destroy even the children. The devil will take glory in feeding perfidiously on the hearts of children. The innocence of childhood will almost disappear. Thus priestly vocations will be lost, it will be a real disaster. Priests will abandon their sacred duties and will depart from the path marked out for them by God." —Our Lady of Good Fortune at Quito, Ecuador, February 2, 1634.

Mother Maria Rafols

". . . The offenses that I have received, and those

that I shall yet receive are many, especially woman, with her immodest dress, her nakedness, her frivolity and her evil intentions. Because of all this, she shall accomplish the demoralization of the family and of mankind. Such shall be the corruption of morality in every social class, and so great [the] unchastity, that My Eternal Father shall be forced to destroy entire cities, should they not reform after this merciful call.

"Ordinarily the corruption of the family always has been the origin of the public calamities and of the destruction of the Christian Faith, for the first purpose of our common enemy is the destruction of the Christian family; once he attains this, the infernal enemy is sure of victory. Therefore, the great evil of these times, and of the even worse than these that shall come, always has been and always shall be to lose the memory and taste of the supernatural life, living only for earthly and sinful things. . . ." —Our Lord to Mother Maria Rafols, Spanish Mystic and Mother Superior, dated 1815 and discovered in 1931. From *The Prophets and Our Times*, Imprimatur 1941, TAN, 1974, p. 187.

Note on Modesty in Tropical Mission Lands

"St. Alphonsus Liguori, Doctor of the Church, admitting that a limited measure of immodest exposure can cease to be a grave snare to people who have grown used to it, adds that those who first introduce it when it is a grave snare, sin gravely, and he makes it clear that there are limits beyond which customariness does not remove the grave snare. (*Theologia Moralis*, Lib. 2, n. 55). The Holy Office under Pius IX favored this view, as may be seen in *Collectanea S. C. de Propaganda Fide*, vol. 1, n. 1061 (Rome, 1907), requiring the adoption of some body coverage, in the interest of modesty, of savages who wish to become Catholic.

"Pope Pius XI had good reasons when he condemned the nudist colony movement as undermining and destroying modesty and shame, which he called 'nature's two protectors of chastity.' He called the use and cult of nudism 'a horrible blasphemy.' This is reported in *l'Osservatore Romano* of March 6, 1935, and in the public press of that time." —From the appendix to an article entitled "Modesty in Fashions" in *Christian Order*, London, January, 1998, p. 56.

Modesty of the Eyes [Custody of the Eyes]

"There are looks which are *grievously sinful*, that offend not only against modesty, but against chastity itself; from such we must evidently abstain. (*Matt.* 5:28). Others there are which are *dangerous*; for instance, to fasten our eyes on persons or things which would of themselves be apt to bring on temptations. Thus Holy Scripture warns us: 'Gaze not upon a maiden: lest her beauty be a stumbling-block to thee.' (*Ecclus.* 9:5). Today, when indecency in dress, exhibitions of the stage and of certain types of drawing-room entertainment create so many dangers, what great care must we not exercise so as not to expose ourselves to sin!

"The earnest Christian who wants to save his soul at all costs goes even further so as to make the danger more remote. He mortifies the sense of sight by repressing idle, curious glances and by duly controlling his eyes in all simplicity without any show of affectation. He takes the opportunity whenever offered of directing his looks towards those things that tend to raise his heart towards God and the Saints, such as holy pictures, statues, churches and crosses." —*The Spiritual Life*, by V. Rev. Adolphe Tanquerey, S.S., D.D., Imprimatur, 1930, TAN, 2000, p. 375.

Notification Concerning Men's Dress Worn by Women

By Giuseppe Cardinal Siri*

Genoa, June 12, 1960

To the Reverend Clergy,
To all Teaching Sisters,
To the beloved sons of Catholic Action,
To Educators intending truly to follow
    Christian Doctrine.[1]

I

The first signs of our late arriving spring indicate that there is this year a certain increase in the use of men's dress by girls and women, even mothers of families. Up until 1959, in Genoa, such dress usually meant the person was a tourist, but now there seems to be a significant number of girls and women from Genoa itself who are choosing, at least on pleasure trips, to wear men's dress (men's trousers).

The extension of this behavior obliges us to take serious thought, and we ask those to whom this Notification is addressed kindly to lend to the problem all the attention it deserves [to receive] from anyone aware of being in any way responsible before God.

---

*This pastoral letter appeared in 1960 in *Rivista Diocesi*, diocesan newspaper of the Diocese of Genoa. This translation from the Italian and the Translator's Notes copyright 1997 by St. Thomas Aquinas Seminary. Used with permission.

We seek above all to give a balanced moral judgment upon the wearing of men's dress by women. In fact, Our thoughts can only bear upon the moral question.[2]

Firstly, when it comes to the covering of the female body, the wearing of men's trousers by women cannot be said to constitute, as such, a grave offense against modesty, because trousers certainly cover more of woman's body than do modern women's skirts.

Secondly, however, clothes, to be modest, need not only to cover the body, but also not to cling too closely to the body.[3] Now it is true that much feminine clothing today clings closer than do some trousers, but trousers can be made to cling closer, in fact generally they do, so the tight fit of such clothing gives us not less grounds for concern than does exposure of the body. So the immodesty of men's trousers on women is an aspect of the problem which is not to be left out of an over-all judgment upon them, even if it is not to be artificially exaggerated either.

II

However, it is a different aspect of women's wearing of men's trousers which seems to us the gravest.[4]

The wearing of men's dress by women affects firstly the woman herself, by changing the feminine psychology proper to women; secondly, it affects the woman as wife of her husband, by tending to vitiate relationships between the sexes; thirdly, it affects the woman as mother of her children by harming her dignity in her children's eyes. Each of these points is to be carefully considered in turn:

A. Male Dress Changes the Psychology of Woman.

In truth, the motive impelling women to wear men's dress is always that of imitating, nay, of competing with the man, who is considered stronger, less tied down, more independent. This motivation shows clearly that male dress is the visible aid to bringing about a mental attitude of being "like a man."[5]

Secondly, ever since men have been men, the clothing a person wears, demands, imposes and modifies that person's gestures, attitudes and behavior, such that from merely being worn on the outside, clothing comes to impose a particular frame of mind on the inside.

Then let us add that a woman wearing man's dress always more or less indicates her reacting to her femininity as though it is inferiority, when in fact it is only diversity. The perversion of her psychology is clearly to be seen.[6]

These reasons, summing up many more, are enough to warn us how wrongly women are made to think by the wearing of men's dress.

B. Male Dress Tends to Vitiate Relationships Between Women and Men.

In truth, when relationships between the two sexes unfold with the coming of age, an instinct of mutual attraction is predominant. The essential basis of this attraction is a diversity between the two sexes, which is made possible only by their complementing or completing one another. If then this "diversity" becomes less obvious because one of its major external signs is eliminated and because the normal psychological structure is weakened, what results is the alteration of a fundamental factor in the relationship.

The problem goes further still. Mutual attraction between the sexes is preceded both naturally and in order of time by that sense of shame which holds the rising instincts in check, imposes respect upon them, and tends to lift to a higher level of mutual esteem and healthy fear everything that those instincts would push onwards to uncontrolled acts. To change that clothing which by its diversity reveals and upholds nature's limits and defense-works is to flatten out the distinctions and to help pull down the vital defense-works of the sense of shame.

It is at least to hinder that sense. And when the sense of shame is hindered from putting on the brakes, then relationships between men and women sink degradingly down to pure sensuality, devoid of all mutual respect or esteem.

Experience is there to tell us that when woman is de-feminized, then defenses are undermined and weakness increases.[7]

C. Male Dress Harms the Dignity of the Mother In Her Children's Eyes.

All children have an instinct for the sense of dignity and decorum of their mother. Analysis of the first inner crisis of children when they awaken to life around them, even before they enter upon adolescence, shows how much the sense of their mother counts. Children are as sensitive as can be on this point. Adults have usually left all that behind them and think no more on it. But we would do well to recall to mind the severe demands that children instinctively make of their own mother, and the deep and even terrible reactions roused in them by observation of their mother's misbehavior. Many lines of later life are here traced out—and not for good—in these early inner dramas of infancy and childhood.

The child may not know the definition of exposure, frivolity or infidelity, but he possesses an instinctive sixth sense to recognize them when they occur, to suffer from them, and to be bitterly wounded by them in his soul.

III

Let us think seriously on the import of everything said so far, even if woman's appearing in man's dress does not immediately give rise to all the upset caused by grave immodesty.

The changing of feminine psychology does fundamental and, in the long run, irreparable damage to the family, to conjugal fidelity, to human affections and to human society.[8] True, the effects of wearing unsuitable dress are not all to be seen within a short time. But one must think of what is being slowly and insidiously worn down, torn apart, perverted.

Is any satisfying reciprocity between husband and wife imaginable if feminine psychology be changed? Or, is any true education of children imaginable, which is so delicate in its procedure, so woven of imponderable factors, in which the mother's intuition and instinct play the decisive part in those tender years? What will these women be able to give their children when they will so long have worn trousers that their self-esteem goes more by their competing with men than by their functioning as women?

Why, we ask, ever since men have been men, or rather since they became civilized—why have men in all times and places been irresistibly borne to make a differentiated division between the functions of the two sexes? Do we not have here strict testimony to the recognition by all mankind of a truth and a law above man?

To sum up, wherever women wear men's dress, it is

to be considered a factor, in the long run, in the tearing apart of human order.

IV

The logical consequence of everything presented so far is that anyone in a position of responsibility should be possessed by a *sense* of *alarm* in the true and proper meaning of the word, a severe and decisive *alarm*.[9]

We address a grave warning to parish priests, to all priests in general and to confessors in particular, to members of every kind of association, to all religious, to all nuns, especially to teaching Sisters.

We invite them to become clearly conscious of the problem so that action will follow. This consciousness is what matters. It will suggest the appropriate action in due time. But let it not counsel us to give way in the face of inevitable change, as though we are confronted by a natural evolution of mankind, and so on!

Men may come and men may go, because God has left plenty of room for the to-and-fro of their free will; but the substantial lines of Nature and the not less substantial lines of Eternal Law have never changed, are not changing [now] and never will change. There are bounds beyond which one may stray as far as one sees fit, but to do so ends in death;[10] there are limits which empty philosophical fantasizing may have one mock or not take seriously, but they [these limits] put together an alliance of hard facts and Nature to chastise anybody who steps over them. And history has sufficiently taught, with frightening proof from the life and death of nations, that the reply to all violators of the outline of "humanity" is always, sooner or later, catastrophe.

From the dialectic of Hegel [German philosopher, 1770-1831] onwards, we have had dinned into our ears what are nothing but fables, and by dint of hearing them so often, many people end up by getting used to them, if only passively. But the truth of the matter is that Nature and Truth, and the Law bound up in both, go their imperturbable way, and they cut to pieces the simpletons who, upon no grounds whatsoever, believe in radical and far-reaching changes in the very structure of man.[11]

The consequences of such violations are not a new outline of man, but disorders, hurtful instability of all kinds, the frightening dryness of human souls, the shattering increase in the number of human castaways, driven long since out of people's sight and mind to live out their decline in boredom, sadness and rejection. Aligned on the wrecking of the eternal norms are to be found the broken families, lives cut short before their time, hearths and homes gone cold, old people cast to one side, youngsters willfully degenerate and, at the end of the line, souls in despair and taking their own lives—all of which human wreckage gives witness to the fact that the "line of God" does not give way, nor does it admit of any adaptation to the delirious dreams of the so-called philosophers![12]

V

We have said that those to whom the present Notification is addressed are invited to take serious alarm at the problem at hand. Accordingly, they know what they have to say, starting with little girls on their mothers' knee.

They know that without exaggerating or turning into fanatics, they will need to limit strictly how far they tolerate women's dressing like men as a general rule.

They know they must never be so weak as to let anyone believe that they turn a blind eye to a custom which is slipping downhill and undermining the moral standing of all institutions.

They, the priests, know that the line they have to take in the confessional, while not holding women's dressing like men to be automatically a grave fault, must be sharp and decisive.[13]

Everybody will kindly give thought to the need for a united line of action, reinforced on every side by the cooperation of all men of good will and all enlightened minds, so as to create a true dam to hold back the flood.

Those of you responsible for souls in whatever capacity understand how useful it is to have for allies in this defensive campaign men of the arts, the media and the crafts. The position taken by fashion design houses, their brilliant designers and the clothing industry is of crucial importance in this whole question. Artistic sense, refinement and good taste, meeting together, can find a suitable but dignified solution as to the dress for women to wear when they must use a motorcycle or engage in this or that exercise or work. What matters is to preserve modesty, together with the eternal sense of femininity, that femininity which, more than anything else, all children will continue to associate with the face of their mother.[14]

We do not deny that modern life sets problems and makes requirements unknown to our grandparents. But we state that there are values more needing to be protected than fleeting experiences, and that for anybody of intelligence there are always good sense and good taste enough to find acceptable and dignified solutions to problems as they come up.[15]

Out of charity, we are fighting against the flattening out of mankind—against the attack upon those differences on which rests the complementarity of man and woman.

When we see a woman in trousers, we should think not so much of her as of all mankind, of what it will be when women will have masculinized themselves for good. Nobody stands to gain by helping to bring about a future age of vagueness, ambiguity, imperfection and, in a word, monstrosities.[16]

This letter of Ours is not addressed to the public, but to those responsible for souls, for education, for Catholic associations. Let them do their duty, and let them not be sentries caught asleep at their post while evil crept in.

—Giuseppe Cardinal Siri
Archbishop of Genoa

Translator's Notes

1. At the end of the Cardinal's Notification, he explains that it is not addressed by him directly to the public at large, but only indirectly, through the Catholic leaders here listed. However, that was in 1960, when the Church still had a framework of leaders. In 1997, those capable by their Faith of responding to the Cardinal's instruction are scattered amongst the public at large, to whom therefore his instruction is fittingly diffused.

2. The Cardinal heads off many objections at the outset when he reminds us by what right he tackles such a subject at all: as a teacher of faith and morals. Who can reasonably deny that clothing (especially, but not only, women's) involves morals and so the salvation of souls?

3. Jeans are now virtually universal. How many women's jeans are not tight-fitting?

4. Trousers on women are worse than mini-skirts, said Bishop de Castro Mayer, because while mini-skirts attack the senses, women's trousers attack man's highest spiritual faculty, the mind. Cardinal Siri explains why, in depth.

5. When women wish to be like men (somebody said that feminists are more scornful than anybody of womanhood), it is up to the men to make women proud of being women.

6. The enormous increase since 1960 in the practice and public flaunting of the vice against nature is surely to be attributed in part to this perversion of psychology.

7. When woman is feminine, she has the strength God gives to her. When she is de-feminized, she has only the strength she gives herself.

8. For an example of this damage, see the relationship between the sexes as portrayed in Rock music.

9. In 1997, can we say the Cardinal was exaggerating?

10. All great art and literature testifies to this moral structure of the universe, which one violates at one's peril and which is as much part of the Natural Order as its physical structure. The plays of Shakespeare are a famous example. The Cardinal is here at the heart of the question.

11. It has been said, "God is ready to forgive always, man sometimes, Nature never."

12. The Cardinal is not just indulging in rhetoric. Pink Floyd's misery is an example of this "human wreckage."

13. How much wisdom and balance there is in all these apparently severe conclusions of the Cardinal!

14. In other words, the femininity of the mother, not of Eve.

15. See note 13, above.

16. In 1997 we see all around us the age of monstrosities, which in 1960 Cardinal Siri was doing his best to prevent. In the Cardinal's own country, Italy, the birthrate has been pushed lowest in all of Europe! Italian youth is devastated. The Cardinal was not listened to *then*. Will he be listened to now?

Selected Bibliography

Andelin, Helen B. *Fascinating Womanhood®*, Updated Edition. Pacific Press, 1965; New York: Bantam Books, a division of Random House, 1992.

Attwater, Donald, General Editor. *A Catholic Dictionary.* New York: Macmillan, 1931, 1961; TAN, 1997.

Baltimore Catechism, various editions.

"Biography of Coco Chanel" www.angelfire.com/ne/lliegirls/chanel/html

Bosco, St. John. *Forty Dreams of St. John Bosco.* Rockford, IL: TAN, 1996.

Civardi, Msgr. Luigi. *How Christ Changed the World: The Social Principles of the Catholic Church.* (Formerly titled *Christianity and Social Justice.*) Trans., Sylvester Andriano. Fresno, CA: Academy Library Guild Press, circa 1961; rpt., TAN, 1991.

"Coco Chanel." www.DiscoverParis.com

Davidson, Rita. *Immodesty: Satan's Virtue.* A Martyrs of Purity Handbook. A publication of Little Flowers Family Apostolates. Lanark, Ontario: Little Flowers Family Apostolates, 2001. www.lffa-ollmpc.com

Dillon, D.D., Monsignor George E. *Grand Orient Freemasonry Unmasked.* Dublin: Gill, 1885; reprint, Palmdale, CA: Christian Book Club, 1999. Imprimatur 1885 and 1950.

"Dressing for a New Millennium," The Holland Sentinel, January 3, 2000. www.thehollandsentinel.net/stories/010300/fea_dressing.html

Garrigou-Lagrange, O.P., Fr. Reginald. *The Three Ages of the Interior Life.* St. Louis, MO: B. Herder Book Co., 1947 (Vol. 1), 1948 (Vol. 2); reprint, Rockford, IL: TAN, 1989.

Gaudiose, Dorothy. *Prophet of the People: A Biography of Padre Pio.* Staten Island, NY: Alba House, 1974.

Gray, John. *Men Are from Mars, Women Are from Venus.* New York: Harper Collins, 1992.

Gresh, Dannah. "'Truth or Bare?' Modesty Tests." March 11, 2004. www.purefreedom.org

Hart, Robert T. *Those Who Serve God Should Not Follow the Fashions.* Pray the Rosary Web Apostolate. www.groups.msn.com/PrayTheRosary

Joseph, Aime. "Coco Chanel: Innovator and Icon." *www.coololdstuff.com / coco.html*

Klepper, Erhard. *Costume through the Ages: Over 1400 Illustrations.* Mineola, NY: Dover Publications, Inc., 1999.

Kunkel, Fr. Bernard A. *Marylike Modesty Handbook of the Purity Crusade of Mary Immaculate.* Original edition, circa 1955; revised edition published as part of *My Life in Prayer Book.* Pittsburgh: Radio Rosary, 1998.

Laver, James. *Costume and Fashion: A Concise History*, 4th Edition. New York: Thames & Hudson, Inc., 1969, 2002.

Lopez, Tracy Tucciarone. "Modesty." www.kensmen.com/catholic/modesty/html

Lopez, Tracy Tucciarone. "Veiling." www.kensmen.com/catholic/theveil.html

Madden, Bro. Charles, O.F.M. Conv. *Freemasonry: Mankind's Hidden Enemy.* Rockford, IL: TAN, 1995.

Martin, Louise. *Immodest Dress: The Mind of the Church.* Monrovia, CA: Catholic Treasures, circa 1995.

McInerny, D. Q. *A Course in Thomistic Ethics.* Elmhurst, PA: The Priestly Fraternity of St. Peter, 1997.

McInerny, D. Q. *Philosophical Psychology.* Elmhurst, PA: The Priestly Fraternity of St. Peter, 1999.

Meyer, Albert G., Archbishop of Milwaukee (later Cardinal Meyer). Pastoral Letter, "Decency and Modesty," May 1, 1956.

Monks of Solesmes, Selected and Arranged by. *The Woman in the Modern World.* (Series: *Papal Teachings*). Boston: Daughters of St. Paul, 1959. (Cited herein as *WMW.*)

Morrow, S.T.D., Most Reverend Louis Laravoire. *My Catholic Faith: A Manual of Religion.* Kenosha, WI: My Mission House, 1949, 1961.

"Rome's Decrees on Modesty in Dress Are Still Victims of 'Conspiracy of Silence.'" Article reprinted from *The Marylike Crusader*, Nov.-Dec., 1963. Marylike Crusade headquartered in Bartelso, IL. This particular reprint published by The Marylike Crusade, P.O. Box 387, Rathdrum, ID 83858.

Tortora, Phyllis G. & Keith Eubanks. *Survey of Historic Costume: A History of Western Dress*, 2nd Edition. New York: Fairchild Publications, 1989, 1994.

van Zeller, Dom Hubert. *Holiness for Housewives.* Manchester, NH: Sophia Institute Press, 1997.

Vennari, John. *The Permanent Instruction of the Alta Vendita: A Masonic Blueprint for the Subversion of the Catholic Church.* Rockford, IL: TAN, 1999.

von Hildebrand, Ph.D., Alice. *The Privilege of Being a Woman*, 4th Edition. Ann Arbor, MI: Sapientia Press of Ave Maria University, 2002, 2004.

von Hildebrand, Dietrich. *The Devastated Vineyard.* Chicago: Franciscan Herald Press, 1973.

WMW—*The Woman in the Modern World.* See Monks of Solesmes.

Dressing with Dignity

1 copy	$10.00	
2 copies	8.00 ea.	16.00
3 copies	7.00 ea.	21.00
5 copies	6.00 ea.	30.00
10 copies or more	5.00 ea.	50.00

U.S. POST/HDLG: If total order=$1-$10, add $3.00; $10.01-$25, add $5.00; $25.01-$50, add $6.00; $50.01-$75, add $7.00; $75.01-$150, add $8.00; orders of $150.01 or more, add $10.00.

Please send me _____ copy (copies) of **Dressing with Dignity**.

☐ Enclosed is my payment in the amount of _____.

☐ Please charge to ☐ Visa ☐MasterCard ☐ Discover

Credit Card No. _____

My credit card expires _____

Account Name _____

Signature _____

Do not send us your card.

Name _____

Street _____

City _____

State _____ Zip _____

Tel. _____ Email _____

TAN BOOKS AND PUBLISHERS, INC.
P.O. Box 424, Rockford, Illinois 61105

1-800-437-5876 • FAX 815-226-7770 • WWW.TANBOOKS.COM

GIVE

DRESSING WITH DIGNITY

To your daughters, granddaughters, nieces, grandnieces, god-children, friends, neighbors, the girl next door, clerks at the store, young women in restaurants, women on the street, high school students, college students, anyone you meet who needs it!!

But above all, give it to leaders and opinion makers . . . to pastors, parish youth directors, teachers, RCIA directors, school principals, high school counselors, etc., etc.

Carry copies with you in your car so you have them on hand at all times. "Together we can change the world, one outfit at a time," as the author puts it—one woman at a time. For this is a book the devil does not want women to read (or men!), does not even want to see published, does not want to see circulated, because **Dressing with Dignity** is a peppy, highly informative, very readable and enjoyable book that delivers an important message on a vital topic that our society desperately needs today!

It is a book that can make an enormous difference in our world, and it is definitely a book that addresses a very serious problem. From Catholic, Protestant, Moslem, Jewish (yes, even Atheist) readers, **Dressing with Dignity** has won acclaim as far and away the best, most effective book on this subject yet to appear. Aimed at women, **Dressing with Dignity**, in Colleen Hammond's gracious and interesting style, scores point after fascinating point that all of us need to know about dressing in a proper, dignified manner. There is no other book quite like it. This is definitely a book whose time has come. But it can only be as effective as the help you and others who are likeminded will give it. Therefore, give **Dressing with Dignity** to those who stand to profit and benefit from it. God will bless you!

Copies	Each	Sh/Hdlg	Total
1 copy	$10.00	+3.00	13.00
2 copies	8.00 ea.	+5.00	21.00
3 copies	7.00 ea.	+5.00	26.00
5 copies	6.00 ea.	+6.00	36.00
10 copies (or more)	5.00 ea.	+6.00	56.00

Illinois residents add 7% sales tax.

TAN BOOKS AND PUBLISHERS, INC.
P.O. Box 424, Rockford, Illinois 61105

1-800-437-5876 • FAX 815-226-7770 • WWW.TANBOOKS.COM

About the Author

A former Miss Michigan National Teenager, actress, model, and a cable network anchor for The Weather Channel, Colleen Hammond lived the American Dream—but found it to be a nightmare. While working in television, she reverted to the Catholic Faith. The moment her first baby was born, she "saw the light" and abandoned her highly successful career to become a stay-at-home mother.

Currently heard as a host of "St. Joseph Radio Presents"— available to 85 million people worldwide on WEWN—Colleen is an award-winning writer, radio and television talk show host, educator and Catholic mother. Acclaimed for her versatility, she delivers an enduring message filled with down-to-earth wisdom, inspiration and humor. Colleen brings a fresh and creative approach to living out the Catholic Faith daily and has helped thousands of people to make positive and virtuous changes in their lives.

A frequent speaker at conferences, retreats and parish events, Colleen Hammond addresses timely topics related to marriage, children, and Catholic values and virtues. Groups appreciate her real-life solutions to tough problems—presented with compassion and warmth in a lively, interactive style. She is also working on a number of other projects.

Colleen, her husband and their four children now live in North Texas.